"Not achieving the results you want or need? Wonder what happened to the communication, cooperation, and collaboration in your organization? It's highly likely your organization is suffering from the affects of stress. In *Mystic Cool*, Don Joseph Goewey explains the source of stress and how to eliminate it... forever. This is the ultimate leadership book!"

Jim Horan, president and CEO, One Page Business Plan Company
and author of *The One Page Business Plan*

"Having read and studied a good deal of modern neuroscience, I am particularly impressed by Don Goewey's brilliant new book, *Mystic Cool*. He makes the brain come alive in his imminently practical and immediately usable book. When people understand what's happening between their ears, they have more power to exercise choice and lead truly outstanding lives. This fact makes *Mystic Cool* a no-brainer choice to read and apply."

Daniel Ellenberg, PhD, consultant, therapist,
and seminar leader, Authentic Leadership Institute

Mystic Cool

A proven approach to transcend stress,
achieve optimal brain function, and maximize
your creative intelligence

Don Joseph Goewey

ATRIA BOOKS
New York London Toronto Sydney

BEYOND WORDS
Hillsboro, Oregon

ATRIA BOOKS

A Division of Simon & Schuster, Inc.
1230 Avenue of the Americas
New York, NY 10020

BEYOND WORDS

20827 N.W. Cornell Road, Suite 500
Hillsboro, Oregon 97124-9808
503-531-8700 / 503-531-8773 fax
www.beyondword.com

Copyright © 2009 by Don Joseph Goewey

Managing editor: Lindsay S. Brown
Editor: Marie Hix
Copyeditor: Ali McCart
Proofreader: Jennifer Weaver-Neist
Design: Devon Smith
Composition: William H. Brunson Typography Services

First Atria Books/Beyond Words hardcover edition April 2009

ATRIA BOOKS and colophon are trademarks of Simon & Schuster, Inc.
Beyond Words Publishing is a division of Simon & Schuster, Inc.

For more information about special discounts for bulk purchases, please contact Simon & Schuster Special Sales at 1-800-456-6798 or business@simonandschuster.com.

The Simon & Schuster Speakers Bureau can bring authors to your live event. For more information or to book an event, contact the Simon & Schuster Speakers Bureau at 866-248-3049 or visit our website at www.simonspeakers.com.

Manufactured in the United States of America

10   9   8   7   6   5   4   3   2   1

Library of Congress Cataloging-in-Publication Data:

Goewey, Don Joseph.
     Mystic cool : a proven approach to transcend stress, achieve optimal brain function, and maximize your creative intelligence / Don Joseph Goewey.
        p.   cm.
     Includes bibliographical references and index.
        1. Stress (Psychology)—Popular works.   2. Anxiety—Popular works.
     3. Neuroplasticity—Popular works.   I. Title.

BF575.S75G58   2009
155.9′042—dc22

                                                                2008046649

ISBN-13: 978-1-58270-227-8
ISBN-10:   1-58270-227-6

The corporate mission of Beyond Words Publishing, Inc.: *Inspire to Integrity*

This book is dedicated to Bonny Meyer

To my grandchildren
Jaden, Kalia, Lilah, Sadie, Gracie, Quinn, and Mia

To their grandchildren and
to the grandchildren of their grandchildren

Contents

Acknowledgments   ix

Introduction by Valerie Land Henderson   xi

Prologue: Up to Me   xv

1. Ordinary Genius   1

2. Dragon, The Primitive Brain   13

3. Apollo, The Neocortex   27

4. Mars, The Emotional Brain   43

5. The Mystical Brain   67

6. Awareness: The Storm   85

7. The Eye of the Storm   107

8. The Neuroplasticity of Practice   119

9. The First Quality of Mystic Cool: Quietly Engaged,
   Fully Present   125

10. The Second Quality of Mystic Cool: Calm and Clear Inside,
    Regardless of Outside   137

11. The Third Quality of Mystic Cool: Connected and
    Connecting   147

12. The Fourth Quality of Mystic Cool: The Whole that
    Transcends the Fragments   165

Epilogue: Never, Never, Never Give Up   175

Addendum: A Simple Practice   179

Notes   183

Index   199

Acknowledgments

As in most long journeys, the distance traveled by *Mystic Cool* required the support of a number of people, all of whom I wish to acknowledge here.

Key to the early effort involved the staff and board of the International Center for Attitudinal Healing including Louise Franklin, Jimmy Pete, Dezorah Smith, Richard Cuadra, Cheryl Geoffrion, Jerry Jampolsky, Jennifer Andrews, Trish Ellis, Lloyd Henderson, Shannon Taylor, Marilyn Robinson, Sharon Pair-Taylor, Joey Roberts, Penelope More, Richard Cohn, Greg Sherwood, John Mays, and Michael Lipson. I especially wish to thank Rick Brandon for his enormous support, practically, emotionally and creatively.

I was also supported by professionals from the world of training and organization development including Dale Biron, Dr. Susannah Baldwin, Andrew Black, Alexandra Jurasin, Valorie Beer, Dr. Lee Jampolsky, Neil Andersen, Jonathan Colton, Marc Verdi, David Goewey, Greg Sherwood, Rinaldo Brutoco and the board of the World Business Academy, and Matthew Mitchell. In addition, I wish to thank my friends Covey Cowan, Terryl Kistler, and Patrick Gleeson for their enormous encouragement during the process. I also want to thank

Rick Brennan and Kimberly St. Clair-Davis of ProAttitude for their tactical and moral support.

I owe so much to Len Brutocao of Brutocao Engineering and Construction and to Dickson Buxton of Private Capital Corporation for their faith in this approach and their willingness to bring it into their companies, where it could be tested.

In transposing ideas and concepts into a readable book, I am indebted to my editor, Valerie Land Henderson, for helping me in my aim to simplify a complex subject into clear ideas through which people could come to see themselves and sense the potential for freedom. I owe much to the help of my beloved partner Louise Franklin for lifting several parts of the book to much higher ground.

I am grateful to my agent, Dr. Barbara Neighbors Deal, for opening doors and introducing me to Beyond Words. I am also fortunate to have such visionary publishers as Cindy Black and Richard E. Cohn, who believed in the Mystic Cool message, and to my managing editor, Lindsay Brown, for her craft, intelligence, and good heart.

And of course, I need to thank my family: my children, David, Brent, Sam, and Hollan; my sisters, Anne Marie and Susie; my brother, Paul; and my niece Jacquie. Thank you for all the pats on the back when I needed them.

I especially wish to thank my mother, Audrey Anne Cochran, for her faith in me and her pride in what I was accomplishing. It saddens me that she died before she could hold the hardcover edition of this book in her hands.

Last and most especially, I wish to thank Bonny Meyer, to whom this book is respectfully and lovingly dedicated. Bonny has contributed so much at every level that matters. Without her support and faith, this book would not be in your hands. And it is her deepest wish that this book is not only in your hands but that it is serving your life in the best way it can.

Introduction

E vident throughout this book are the influence and contributions of those who have gone before in the fields of psychology, psychiatry, and science, though it is certain *Mystic Cool* will have its own unique place in a nonlinear continuum of all three.

On the subject of human nature, well-known American psychologist Carl R. Rogers wrote: "... the basic nature of the human being, when functioning freely, is constructive and trustworthy. For me this is an inescapable conclusion from a quarter-century of experience in psychotherapy. When we are able to free the individual from defensiveness, so that he is open to the wide range of his own needs, as well as the wide range of environmental and social demands, his reactions may be trusted to be positive, forward-moving, constructive." This same philosophy is reflected by Goewey as he emphasizes the power of individuals to influence the quality of their own experience.

When a writer takes on the task of communicating a new vision in an area that has been written about comprehensively, inevitably he will face the limitations of language. It is the age-old problem of new wine in old wineskins. Goewey has succeeded in elucidating his viewpoint brilliantly. He has researched his material extensively, and the entire book is informed with the latest data available in the field of neuroscience.

Introduction

Readers of this book will benefit from the simple yet profound knowledge to be found here and, in addition, will be enriched by the very personal account given of Goewey's life journey to this point. The hard-won compassion he has learned to give to himself and others is mirrored in the very nature of this book and its intent: to help sufferers free themselves from the chains of chronic stress and, in the process, from the tyranny of self-blame.

Although it will be useful to the professional, the book's primary value, I believe, will be to the ordinary individual seeking a pathway to transcending the anxiety and pressures of daily life. Goewey shows simply and clearly how this can be achieved, and is thoroughly convincing in his admonition of its importance.

Wolfgang Amadeus Mozart wrote, "Neither a lofty degree of intelligence, nor imagination, nor both together, go to the making of genius. Love, love, love, that is the soul of genius." I believe this book to be an act of love and of genius.

Valerie Land Henderson

Valerie Land Henderson was assistant to Carl R. Rogers, PhD, coedited with Howard Kirschenbaum *The Carl Rogers Reader* and *Carl Rogers: Dialogues*. She was a resident fellow and former director of the Center for Studies of the Person, which was cofounded by Carl Rogers. Valerie also held positions with the Center for Cross-Cultural Communication and the Cener for Attitidunal Healing.

*… a new turning, a new attitude, an inner change,
a liberation from all futile concerns …*

Thomas Merton

Prologue: Up to Me

*In fourteen months I only smiled once, and I didn't do it
consciously. Somebody's got to find your trail.
I guess it must be up to me.*

Bob Dylan, "Up to Me"

Twenty years ago, circumstances converged with my sinking attitude
to create a perfect storm of stress. Ironically, it all occurred as my
career path appeared to be approaching a summit. Just a year and a half
earlier, I had convinced some of the brightest minds in medicine that I
was the best of the candidates vying for the position of lead executive
officer in the Department of Medicine at Stanford University. This was
the largest department in the university and a potential stepping stone
to greater things. Everyone close to me was quite impressed when the
position was offered to me.

I remember the first day I drove to my job, passing the pasture land
where Leland Stanford once grazed his cattle, turning up Pasteur Drive
toward the towering oak that fronts the magnificent sandy colored
edifice of the medical school. The great fountain at the entrance was
spewing streams of water in the air that the wind fanned into a veil
through which the building's stone glimmered. Huge copper bowls
with red and yellow vines spilling over the sides hung between the high
columns, adorning the simple, almost austere line of the building. That
day I thought I was entering Camelot.

It did not take long for that illusion to be dispelled. The place was
anything but Camelot. This is not to say working at the medical school

was uninspiring. Working with world-class intellects elevated my own thinking and skills. It taught me how to work more effectively with complexity, to be brutally honest with facts, and to identify specious arguments seeking easy solutions. It also exposed me to science, a discipline I had avoided like the plague when I was in school. At Stanford, I came to love science, and for that I am forever grateful. At the same time, it occurred to me that these world-class intellects had world-class egos, and I had a difficult time getting them to cooperate with our strategic plan. Fault finding was rampant and mistakes severely punished, which is, of course, understandable in the field of medicine. But colleagues seemed to relish others' mistakes. One man's loss was another's gain, and it created an atmosphere of distrust. At least, these were my judgments at the time.

The environment was especially hard on women, even for those who held advanced medical degrees. I will never forget the day, early in my tenure, when, returning to my office from a meeting, I observed a female medical resident standing to the side of the department's front door and crying. When I asked her what was wrong, she said, "I just don't fit here," and ran off. I was beginning to come to the same conclusion. I sensed I was in the wrong place and feared it was beginning to show. I didn't have the courage to leave the job, however, not with a wife and four children to support. I was also afraid of what my friends and family would think of me. They had celebrated me for landing the job, and I worried they would think ill of me if I couldn't make it work.

As stressful as the job seemed at the time, my anxiety about it and life in general was far worse. You might be wondering why you should read a book about transcending stress written by someone who managed his own stress so poorly. My answer is: *who better than one who has crossed the terrain?* And the terrain of my fear and the stress it embodied extended beyond the workplace. In those days I was afraid most of the time, though I was not aware of it. I was afraid of what people thought of me and of lulls in our conversations. I was afraid of the bills on my desk, the checks I wrote, and the money I borrowed. I was afraid of failing, especially when I was apparently succeeding.

Prologue

I feared the small stabs of pain in my chest, the swollen lymph nodes that occasionally appeared in the necks of my children when they caught colds, and the odd click or clack in a machine I depended on. I was afraid of affection, intimate moments, and the unhappiness I saw in my wife's eyes. I approached most situations feeling at risk, as if someone were going to see through me, incriminate me, and haul me off. A friend of mine jokes that sometimes when he goes to an ATM to retrieve cash, he half expects the machine to open wide for a cop to step out and cuff him for the crime of impersonating an honest man. That captures something of my anxiety. I was living a kind of self-imposed tyranny from which I was in flight. I was constantly on the run, rarely at ease, never free. It is what Rollo May called "a nameless and formless uneasiness."[1]

The uneasiness exacerbated into full-blown anxiety when the university placed me on probation with ninety days to prove myself. As the deadline approached, my anxiety turned to dread and my self-confidence began to drop, undermining my ability to turn the corner.

Søren Kierkegaard, the great philosopher, wrote:

No Grand Inquisitor has in readiness such terrible tortures as has anxiety. No spy knows how to attack more artfully the man he suspects, choosing the instant when he is weakest, nor knows how to lay traps where he will be caught and ensnared, as anxiety knows how. No sharp-witted judge knows how to interrogate, to examine the accused, as anxiety does, which never lets him escape, neither by diversion nor by noise, neither at work nor at play, neither by day nor by night.[2]

On the appointed day, the axe fell. I was fired. Nine days later I was diagnosed with a brain tumor. As if this weren't enough, the strain of dealing with all of it expanded the cracks in my marriage instead of bringing us closer together. As hard as my wife and I tried, we just could not bridge the gap that had grown between us. I do not think I have ever felt more alone or more lost. My mental state oscillated between abject terror and complete numbness. I was beginning to lose faith in life.

Prologue

The good news was that the tumor was benign and slow growing. The bad news was its size and location. The tumor was large, compressing the fifth, seventh, and eighth cranial nerves, leading to an unhappy prognosis. I could lose half my hearing, suffer impaired balance, and sustain paralysis on the left side of my face. I was thirty-eight at the time, and the medical judgment came as quite a blow. How was I supposed to restart my career, staggering into interviews on a cane and pitching my prospects with a half-frozen face? It was evident to me that my life, as I had known it, was over and my family was doomed to live in poverty.

My connections at the medical school helped me find the best neurosurgeon, although he was not immediately available. Medically, it did not matter since the tumor was slow growing. The delay was a relief, the only relief I had felt in months. I was in no hurry for facial paralysis or a stumbling gait. Having to wait proved to be a blessing. As strange as it may sound, it gave me time to agonize my way to the bottom of my despair, which I reached a week before surgery. It was a cold, gray day. I was alone at home and went outside to the deck to smoke a cigarette and gaze at the view of the hills, hoping to calm my anxiety. But my anxiety only worsened as I reacted to the images of the calamitous future fear painted in my mind. Fear quickly eroded the fragile ledge of safety to which my sanity clung, dropping me into a hollow that spiraled down and down, into a dark cavern of the mind. The more I fell, the darker it got. The darker it got, the more frightened I became until I was lost in panic. It was a nightmare. I did not know what to do to arrest the psychological fall, other than to surrender to the experience. As I did, my terror worsened. It was unbearable, and at some point my conscious mind began to recede inwardly toward a vanishing point, where I seemed to disappear.

Then, like the phoenix rising out of the ash, my conscious mind came back to life. My mind felt emptied, as if cleansed, and curiously spacious, like the soft blue sky after a storm. Everything was quiet and miraculously expansive. Gradually the stillness became palpable and vibrant, like the first awakenings of spring. The stillness surrounded and permeated my being and, for the first time in a very long time, I felt at peace. I relaxed into it completely, the way we relax into the relief of pain. As I did I began to feel loved, by whom or what I cannot say. Perhaps it was just me loving myself for the first time. Perhaps it was only the simple relief and gratitude of having reached safety.

But I was not thinking about it at that moment. I was taken over by the experience of feeling loved, which gradually came to rest in my heart as compassion. I felt compassion for everyone who suffers, including me. The sincerity of my compassion seemed to heal an old sorrow, and I started to cry for the first time in God knows how long. These tears of sorrow released a feeling of gladness and wonder for the adventure and privilege of being alive. When I took my next breath, it felt like the breath of life. When I opened my eyes and looked at the world around me, the first conscious thought I had was that I was OK. This was followed by the recognition that I had always been OK and would always be so. My usual cynicism did not stand up to argue with this feeling. That *all shall be well and all manner of things shall be well* appeared self-evident.

I looked down at my hand, at the cigarette pinched between my fingers, and saw that it had only burned down halfway. It was hard to fathom, given that the experience I had just been through felt like an eternity. When my personality was back intact, I did a reality check. *Do I have a brain tumor?* The answer was yes. *Is the prognosis still the same?* Again, the answer was yes. *Am I about to join the ranks of the unemployed?* Yes to this as well. *Is my marriage on the rocks?* Yes, yes, yes to everything. Yet I still felt I would be fine. I felt at peace inside, despite the difficult circumstances I faced.

The experience stayed with me; the following week was bliss. I did not think much or talk much, and I did not worry. My anxiety was gone. The chairman of the department was kind enough to allow me to continue in my position until the surgery and, afterwards, to take six weeks of paid medical leave. I hadn't intended to go into the office, but now I actually wanted to be there. My peaceful attitude cast everything in a positive, optimistic light, and I guess I wanted to put it to the test. The dean had once called the medical school "this godforsaken place,"

Prologue

and I wanted to see if my new outlook could stand up to the stress and strain it had caused me. To my great joy, peace passed the test. The usual stressors no longer bothered me. My heart opened to people whom I had perceived as enemies and, just a week earlier, had blamed for my demise. I now realized most of my perceptions had been fabricated in my head, and I wanted to give my head every chance to heal. I worked right up to a few days before the surgery, and during that entire time, as I recall, I did not entertain one negative thought.

One day, a couple of weeks prior to surgery, the executive in the Department of Psychiatry paid me a visit. His name was Karl and he was moving over to the Dean's Office to head up human resources. This meant his position was available. It was Karl's impression that I had been given a raw deal in Medicine, and he thought Psychiatry was a better fit for me. If I was open to it, he said he was willing to arrange an interview with Psychiatry's chairman. Karl and I barely knew each other and there was no reason for him to intervene, other than to correct something that struck him as unfair. I did interview for the position and, as I was packing my suitcase to go to the hospital, the chairman of Psychiatry phoned and offered me the job. Naturally, I accepted on the spot. *All shall be well and all manner of things shall be well,* I thought to myself as I hung up the phone. Then I nodded in gratitude to Karl's good heart. I felt blessed, as if a legion of angels was looking after me.

When I checked into the hospital, I was as confident as Michael Jordan before a championship game. The surgery was a total success. It lifted my neurosurgeon's reputation to new heights. The only disability I came away with was a 20 percent loss of hearing. The one problem not solved was my marriage. A year later my wife and I divorced. It was painful, but compassion eventually got us through it.

The Department of Psychiatry did indeed turn out to be a better fit. In my youth I had the great privilege of working with the preeminent American psychologist Carl R. Rogers, and felt I was in my element. The department was an exciting place to be, particularly at that time, when the theory of the mind–body connection was just

Prologue

developing. I was easily distracted from my executive duties. How could I not be? I had an insider's view of the work of some of the giants in their fields, including William Dement, the father of sleep medicine; Karl Pribram, who developed the holonomic brain model of cognitive function; David Spiegel, a leader in psychosomatic research; and Irvin Yalom, who wrote the classic text on group psychotherapy. Once, while cleaning out an overstuffed closet, I even unearthed two lost reels of audio recordings of Jane Goodall discussing primatology with her research fellows.

As much as I enjoyed working in the department, the job felt temporary. More and more, I thought of leaving the university. It was like a way station between where I no longer belonged and where I wanted to be. The peace I had experienced on the other side of terror that day out on the deck had changed me. I kept imagining myself working in an organizaiton that helped people transform the same kind of pain I had experienced that day. I did not know if any such place even existed, only that I felt drawn to find one.

One day, while participating in a meeting with the chairman and the division chiefs, an odd thing happened. At the end of arguing some point I was advancing, I felt my mind drift off. In my mind's eye I saw myself twenty years later, still sitting at this same table, participating in the *conflit du jour*, bored with it. Worse, I was filled with regret for having let the life I was meant to live pass me by. It seemed more than a daydream. It was lucid, enough so that when I returned to the present meeting, I was rattled. I felt as if something was telling me to get up from the table, right then and there, go to my office, and write my resignation. It seemed clear that if I slept on it, when I woke up it would be twenty years later. It was now or never. With my heart pounding, I stood up, excused myself from the meeting, and made my way back to my office to do the bravest thing I have ever done. Bravery and stupidity are indistinguishable at moments like this. In the end, it comes down to a leap of faith, which was the leap I took. I wrote the letter of resignation, made it effective immediately, and then changed it to effective in ninety days. This eased the awful pounding in my heart.

Prologue

Three months later, I left the security of steady employment and stepped out alone into a cold, unfriendly world, with little in the way of savings. My only compass was an inner vision. For a year, I searched for the place I was looking for. When my money ran out, I worked part-time in a factory and borrowed money from my best friend. But I could not find anything that matched what I had envisioned. It was discouraging, but just when I was considering giving up, I found what I had envisioned. It was a nonprofit organization devoted to helping people face the psychological and spiritual challenges of serious illness and dying. The agency, located in Marin County just across the Golden Gate Bridge, was internationally recognized for its approach. I had not heard of it; though, at that point it had been around for fifteen years.

The Center for Attitudinal Healing or "the Center," as it used to be called by clients and volunteers, was founded in 1975 by the respected psychiatrist and bestselling author Gerald Jampolsky, MD, and Patsy Robinson, a woman who could take a vision and make it work in the world. Its clients came from every walk of life and every age group—from parents who had lost children to people diagnosed with life-threatening illness. Many faced the most stressful situations any of us will ever face. At one point, the Center even worked with refugees of war who had lost everything. The Center's core principle reflected precisely my life-changing experience out on the deck; it defined health as inner peace, and healing as letting go of fear. It also had created a peer-support, community-building model, similar to a model I had worked with during my days with Dr. Carl R. Rogers. Its programs depended entirely on a corps of two hundred volunteers, trained and mentored by staff, who delivered services to clients free of charge.

The atmosphere of this organization was humble. It was housed in an old warehouse in Tiburon, on the docks at the north end of San Francisco Bay. The furniture was old, the building rustic, and drawings by children hung on the walls. Yet the agency was clean and tidy, and alive with a joyful energy. It was a community of service extending a relationship of unconditional respect to one and all. Everyone, young and old, was considered both student and teacher. The curriculum was simple and

Prologue

direct: learning to let go of fear in whatever form it manifested. People came from all over the world to visit the Center. Professors, physicians, and therapists came to study, ordinary folks of every persuasion came to lend a hand, poor and rich alike gave money, and there were even a few seekers who came on pilgrimage to find the meaning of life. All were put to work. Upon return to their communities, more than a hundred of these people established centers of their own. This small point of light was mother to a global community dedicated to letting go of fear.

In the process, it had invented one of the important community mental health models of our time. Community mental health was my field, and it was exciting to see what these people were doing. Their model was every bit as effective as AA (Alcoholics Anonymous), and for many of the same reasons. It was people sitting in a circle, guided by practical principles, beginning with equality, and facilitating a sense of connection that can be genuinely healing.

For a month I spent all my available time hanging out at the Center to see if it truly was the place I was looking for. I bought and read many of the books in its bookstore, got to know Patsy Robinson and the staff, and learned all I could about its programs. It *was* the place I was seeking. Like so many other people, I ended up falling in love with this community. Eventually I was recruited to cofacilitate the HIV/AIDS support group. That group delivered many blessings, one of which was a job. Through my cofacilitator, I learned of an opening for the executive director position at a local AIDS agency; I applied and was hired.

The epidemic was at its height. For the next three years I worked with a band of saints, mavericks, angels, rogues, and heroes to serve gay and straight men and women, children, sex workers, and addicts—in short, anyone and everyone infected with HIV. The staff and volunteers at this agency were some of the finest people I have ever known and perhaps some of the best who have walked the Earth; and they needed to be. They were up against nearly total devastation.

The image that etched the deepest impression in my memory was the apartment building where a coworker of mine lived. It was once a village of gay people, living, loving, and supporting each other. In the

Prologue

good days, before AIDS, they shared each other's joys. They nursed each other through flus, colds, and emotional upheavals, and lent a hand with heavy chores. They shared Thanksgiving, Christmas, birthdays, funerals, and whatever else there is to celebrate or grieve. They took pleasure in each other's company and looked out for one another. In short, they were a neighborhood. After the plague hit, there was nearly no one left in that building. For a while, it was like a ghost town.

I will also never forget the unbelievably sick and wasted bodies in hospice houses and hospital wards. I did not know that a human being could get that sick and suffer that much. But, as much as anything, I will also never forget the way the human spirit shone through all the hardship. It came through in the smile lighting up a withered face, and in the resilience of a caregiver who, over and over again, transcended heartache and discouragement to be present, kind, and unfettered in handling the next thing that needed to be done. The tears and laughter of the people fighting the epidemic sprang from a deeper place, as did their kindness and compassion. And who can forget the people who mobilized the research to produce the medicines that changed the disease from terminal to chronic? I sometimes think that the people fighting AIDS are the meek who will inherent the Earth. They reveal to me the emotional and spiritual intelligence I believe will be necessary, if we are to take the next step in the evolution of human culture.

Three years later, I left the AIDS agency to become the executive director of the Center on the docks of Tiburon. The experience was equally as rich. In the Center's support groups, workshops, and counseling programs, I worked with hundreds of people who demonstrated the capacity to make a profound shift in attitude to change their experience entirely, regardless of how dire their situation. Some made the shift quickly; others took more time. But in the twelve years I worked at the Center, I cannot recall anyone who did not make it home. By *home* I mean the experience of peace—the experience that begins where fear ends and grows into a state of mind that makes human beings larger than circumstances. These people helped me to realize the possibility of living in the world without fear, which is not to say living without fears

Prologue

(plural). They faced their fears every day, meeting them with a quality of presence that allowed them to embrace their losses and difficulties, and eventually to transcend them.

There are two women I met who, for me, epitomize the transformation people are capable of making. When I think life has dealt me a bad hand, remembering these women lifts my heart, straightens my spine, and raises my head.

○ ○ ○

The first person was a client at the Center in Argentina. Her name is Pilar. Pilar was a thalidomide baby, born with no arms and severe stunting of growth as a result of her mother being prescribed the drug during pregnancy. Abused, neglected, and tossed aside, she felt like a victim most of her life, bitterly blaming her parents and the medical profession for her misfortune. When she reached adulthood, she was released into a world that was largely repelled by her. If anyone has the right to be angry at life, it is Pilar, and for a long time she was very angry.

With the help of the Center, she began to transcend her fate and the emotional storms it made of her mind. She began to reclaim her life, moment by moment, through the trial-and-error practice of building a peaceful, forgiving attitude. Gradually, Pilar rescued her future from the limited and limiting existence that fear, pessimism, and anger recycled. What eventually emerged through her perseverance was Pilar, as a whole person, alive and free, with the strength, dignity, and intelligence to move mountains—and move mountains she did. She fulfilled a dream that most thought impossible. She became an artist, painting with her feet. She went on to become a wonderful artist and is now considered one of Argentina's national treasures.

I am a proud owner of two of her paintings. The time I spent with Pilar was short but inspiring, even though we exchanged few words. She speaks Spanish, and I do not, but it did not matter. Her face itself was a work of art, illuminated by an attitude that communicated more than words can. "What a humble lesson it is to see such a person," stated Dr. Alberto Loizaga, a psychiatrist and founder of the Center in

Prologue

Argentina. "To witness a person who does not feel victimized, but rather feels a passion for life and the expression of it through art."[3]

The second woman is named Lubie. At the time we met, she was a refugee of the Bosnian War. She attended a workshop we conducted in Zagreb, Croatia, at the height of that horrible war. In contrast to Pilar, whose breakthrough occurred over a period of months, Lubie's happened in a matter of days.

The workshop was part of a program funded by the U.S. State Department to help war refugees cope with the post-traumatic stress that resulted from the unspeakable brutality they had suffered. Lubie was the one person out of three hundred attending the workshop who caught my eye. I still remember watching her come into the room and take a seat in the third row on the outside aisle. She was dressed in black, head to toe, as if in mourning. Sunglasses hid her eyes, and she wore a scarf pulled tight around her head. She did not remove her scarf or the sunglasses and sat motionless throughout the morning, arms folded across her chest, looking at me as I conducted the workshop. The only clue I had to her affect was a downturned mouth that did not change, even when something humorous happened.

When we broke for lunch, I did not expect her to return. As I opened the afternoon session, however, there she was, sitting in the same seat. She now wore neither scarf nor sunglasses, and I could see the deep grief in her eyes. I was surprised again when she returned the next day. Twice that day and the next, we broke into small discussion groups and, as it turned out, Lubie was assigned to the group I was facilitating. In the safety of these groups, she gradually opened up emotionally, revealing some of the tragic experiences she had kept locked inside. She talked about her pain, cried over it, and as she gradually came to accept it, her suffering eased. In the last session, she was much calmer and was a source of support to others in the small group.

Witnessing such healing and its resilience is always astonishing. "The irony is," stated Daniel Siegel, MD, director of the Mindfulness Awareness Research Center at UCLA, "that once you are able to define your boundaries you actually get freedom."[4] It is as Eckhart Tolle described: "The moment you completely accept your nonpeace, your nonpeace becomes transmuted into peace."[5]

Although it was the dead of winter, on the last day of the workshop Lubie appeared in a colorful silk outfit that brought a touch of spring into the room. On this day, she stood up in front of three hundred people and stated that before the workshop she thought she had lost her life. She thought the war had taken her life from her and had left her to live the rest of her days in an empty, loveless shell that reverberated with pain. She stated that over the course of the last three days, everything had changed. In the workshop, she felt safe enough to feel what she had to feel, to see what she needed to see, and eventually to challenge the dark voices of the mind that had drained the joy and peace from her. She then began to cry, but she described her tears as joyful. It was a profound moment of healing for everyone at the workshop. A year later, I had coffee with Lubie in Zagreb and she had not relapsed into the empty persona the war had made of her for a time. Lubie is an example of how quickly people can shift when they are ready.

Often the term *fact of life* is used to refer to a condition imposed by the world over which we have no control. In these two people, peace transcends the facts. Peace, as a dynamic way of being, is the inner strength that makes us larger than circumstances, even larger than anything the world does to us. Fear is the way we lose that strength and power.

Sometime prior to the end of my tenure at the Center, my friend Larry Stupski challenged me to create a program that could alleviate stress, so work could be healthier, more enjoyable and rewarding, leading to greater success. Larry served as president and COO of Charles Schwab during the thirteen-year period of rapid growth that established the company. Larry views stress and the interpersonal dysfunction it generates as a major block to building a company that will last. I shared his point of view and became fascinated with the proposition that there might actually be a solution to stress in the workplace. As I investigated the literature, I found, not surprisingly, that Larry's view was accurate. Generally, the American workplace can be an unhealthy, stressful environment that is damaging to people and organizations. It negatively affects personal performance, teamwork, and motivation, ultimately cutting profitability. It also affects families and relationships outside of work because people take stress home. Most of us recognize it, most of us feel it, and according to a number of studies, most of us wind up dissatisfied with our jobs and lives because of stress. The problem is no one seems to know what to do about it.

I also investigated the available research in neuroscience by reading scores of studies and books. Over the last ten years, neuroscience has had one breakthrough after another in understanding what makes us tick. By and large, what I learned can be summarized thus: Stress is fear, peace is power. Fear is the biological trigger for a stress reaction. Too much stress debilitates higher brain function, and chronic stress makes the brain incapable of sustaining peak performance, cultivating positive relationships, and staying healthy. Obviously, peace is the direct opposite of fear and stress. A dynamically peaceful attitude translates, neurologically, into optimal brain function and regenerative processes that can reverse the trouble stress causes. Neurologically, success is inner peace and succeeding is letting go of fear. And there is a bonus. A dynamically peaceful attitude also generates a more fulfilling experience of life. The psychological term for it is *flow*.

○　○　○

In short, peace represents a brain operating at its absolute best. It generates the brain function needed to succeed at every level of life. Fear represents a brain toxic with stress hormones. It was clear that Larry was correct. We had a solution to the problem, not just for the workplace as Larry suggested, but for parents as well as spouses, students as well as teachers. In short, our solution would work for anyone and everyone who wanted to transcend stress and all the trouble it causes.

Five years later, my research and development efforts have culminated in the formation of a human performance firm called ProAttitude, which helps people reach this optimal state of mind. This book summarizes all that I learned about a dynamically peaceful attitude— the incalculable gift it bestows—and defines a process for attaining it.

1
Ordinary Genius

How beauteous mankind is!
O Brave new world that has such people in't!

William Shakespeare

The most remarkable system in all of biology is, at this moment, reading this book. It has been gently turning the pages, analyzing the information, perhaps arguing with it, responding emotionally, integrating, associating, extrapolating, and ultimately evaluating the book's relevance.

You are the most remarkable system in all of biology.[1] You are the greatest miracle on Earth. You possess nature's greatest single achievement, the human brain. You have the power to direct it with the "most complex set of processes in the universe, the mind."[2] As you use this power, however you use it, you inevitably create your experience of life.

THE GOOD LIFE

The evolution of the human brain was a special event in nature. The swiftness with which natural selection evolved the human brain is unparalleled. It is nothing short of spectacular that so many mutations in so many genes were acquired so quickly.[3] The neocortex was the last part of the brain to evolve. Research at Princeton has confirmed previous studies showing that the neocortex grew rapidly over the course of evolution, expanding from 16 percent of the brain in insect-eaters to 80 percent in humans,[4] setting human beings apart from all other creatures. Nature wanted human beings to be incredibly smart and she wanted it to happen in a hurry. This expansion in size produced everything we think of as intelligence. Nature wasted no time in wiring our brains with the circuitry for a highly creative, intensely social, and deeply emotional mind. The more science studies the neurological, psychological, and spiritual dimensions of the brain becoming the mind, the more it seems that nature intended to free us from toil to know joy and, through joy, to contribute to the ascent of consciousness.

By *joy*, I am referring to the delight we experience when we stretch our talent, knowledge, and skill along lines of excellence. It is the joy of testing, discovering, and then fulfilling our innate potential. This is how the ancient Greeks defined joy. Aristotle called it the "good life" (*eudaimonia*), which defines a state of flourishing. By this he meant "being well and doing well."[5] It is the phenomenon of our positive inner state causing a positive effect in the world. It is living fully and being at peace, meaning we enjoy our work and our life. It means we are at peace with ourselves, comfortable in our own skin, comfortable with other people, as well as possessing the ability to remain calm and clear-headed in a crisis.

For the classical Greeks, peace and joy were not spiritual as much as practical virtues that allow humanity to function fully and to ultimately offer what is uniquely within it to contribute. It seems they intuitively understood what neuroscience is just now discovering through high-tech instrumentation: that peace and joy represent an internal state of consciousness that lifts brain function to its absolute best. The Greeks used their optimal brain function to establish art, science, philosophy, commerce, and democracy to build a civilization that lasted six hundred years and serves as the foundation on which Western culture rests. Lofty achievement is precisely what nature intended.

As wonderful as all this might sound, for many the journey has been anything but joyful. The fact that nature wired us for creativity means we are free to create misery as well as joy, consequences as well as rewards. Our creative nature is often obscured in unhappiness and disappointment, in stress and strain, when these experiences harden into the belief that we are victims of the world. And this creative gift is not only a matter of what we are born with; it is a force we must discover, nurture, and direct for ourselves. "I am the decisive element," stated Johann Wolfgang von Goethe, Germany's greatest man of letters. "It is my personal approach that creates the climate. It is my daily mood that makes the weather. I possess tremendous power to make life miserable or joyous. In all situations, it is my response that decides whether a crisis is escalated or de-escalated."[6]

Often, as we take on the world, we encounter adversity, conflicts, and prejudice that seem to block our way. This can make us anxious, angry, or pessimistic, with one emotion playing off the other, eventually producing a predisposition that Rollo May described as "a vague, persistent uncertainty and helplessness."[7] The word *stressful* captures it. Amplify uncertainty and helplessness and it can intensify into a storm of stress and negativity that fragments the mind, dampens enthusiasm, and shakes self-confidence. It is a far cry from living the good life. Rather, it is a stressful life in which we feel besieged by our work, our challenges, and even our families. In workshops and coaching sessions I conduct, it is common for people to say they cannot remember when they last felt joy or were at peace.[8] They can immediately recall the last time they were angry or depressed, or frozen by the fear of failure, but not at peace. They do not think job performance, success, or the pursuit of excellence might depend on a joyful, peaceful attitude. These people tend to think the good life happens away from work or, sadly, is something that has passed them by.

As you will see, neurologically, joy and peace have everything to do with achieving meaningful success in life at every level. We can forget how peace and joy feel, but no one is devoid of these emotions. They are embedded in the neural circuitry of the brain. Like any human ability, they develop with use. As we consistently flex these positive emotions, brain structure develops that eventually ignites a force of consciousness that makes us larger than circumstances. We come out of the storm into the eye, where the climate of peace and joy is conducive to the ordinary genius we were born to realize. Peace and joy can be our way of being, our everyday experience, instead of an infrequent episode of ambiguous origin between storms of anxiety.

The first step in transcending the storm and reaching the eye is acknowledging the enormous gift of creative power encased in our brain. We can start by asking: what if Nobel Laureate Erik Kandel and other investigators are correct in concluding that each of us possesses the most remarkable system in biology along with the ability to direct it with the most complex set of processes in the universe? If we quietly permit ourselves to believe Kandel enough to feel the power in the words, we might experience an expansion of our own consciousness, dissolving the boundaries of limited thinking. The more power we give to this thought—the more completely we believe that this thought has power—the more power it will have.[9] In this state of mind, we might start to feel bold with possibility, and in our boldness we might sense, as Goethe sensed, "the genius, power, and magic in it."[10] Even a glimpse of this would produce joy in our hearts. If the experience extended further, we might begin to feel inspired by what we know we can do, but have not yet done, or by what we have dreamed of doing that entreats us still. We may even feel compelled to seize this very moment and begin it.

> You see things; and you say, "Why?"
> But I dream things that never were; and I say, "Why not?"
> George Bernard Shaw

The aim of this book is to compel and then to support us in vacating the storm, where we have no real power, and to enter the eye, where the genius, power, and magic of what we are can grow. In the eye, we regain the capacity for as many as seven separate forms of intelligence. These forms of intelligence are archetypal, representing exceptional human abilities—the poet, the scientist, the composer, the

4

sculptor, the athlete, the teacher, and the mystic in every one of us. For example, marketing wizards and great leaders tap the linguistic intelligence of the poet. Strategic planners, engineers, and craftsmen tap the logic and mathematical intelligence of the scientist. Parents, salesmen, and teachers exercise interpersonal intelligence, while mystics, clergy, and psychologists tap intrapersonal intelligence. When we deconstruct a task we are performing, we find that we are accessing more than one form of intelligence, even in simple tasks. "Every normal individual," wrote Howard Gardner of Harvard University, "possesses varying degrees of each of these intelligences, but the ways in which intelligences combine and blend are as varied as the faces and the personalities of individuals."[11]

> **That is happiness: to be dissolved into something complete and great.**
> **Willa Cather**

From time to time, each of us has experienced the glory of ordinary genius when attempting to accomplish something meaningful that stretches our abilities. The usual storm of demands, pressures, and doubts may have been present at the outset, but by subtle twists and turns, we managed to slip past the storm and locate the eye, where the pressure to produce became the challenge to excel. As we settled in, an effortless flow of intelligence took over, sweeping us along in its inevitable current. Our mind became clear and worked with precision. Time stood still. We felt exhilarated and were able to channel, focus, and conserve our enthusiasm, maintaining a high level of energy. Gradually we began to exhibit surprising mastery over the task at hand, preserving a vision of the whole even as we attended to details. Pieces fell effortlessly into place, as if the dots were connecting themselves. Our sense of the whole was expanded as wider possibilities emerged. Working in this way did not feel like work at all. Rather, it became a rewarding labor of love. It is likely, at the end of such an experience, that we felt a "deep sense of enjoyment that ... [became] a landmark in memory for what life should be like."[12]

I don't like work—no man does—but I like what is in the work—
the chance to find yourself. Your own reality—for yourself,
not for others—what no other man can ever know.

Joseph Conrad

When this way of working becomes a way of being, intelligence and beauty flow into the effort we make, whether we are building a company, teaching a class, or doing the laundry. The quality of the experience renders quality in the result, even if it's only in the whiteness of a washed pocket-handkerchief, as D. H. Lawrence wrote in a poem.[13] Few of us have managed to make this flow of intelligence an everyday experience. "How embarrassing," wrote the eminent theologian Abraham Joshua Heschel, "for man to be the greatest miracle on Earth and not to understand it! How embarrassing for man to live in the shadows of greatness and to ignore it."[14]

This beautiful mind that can spring from near infinite points of light in our brain is like a glistening jewel we locked in a safe so long ago that we forgot the combination. What caused us to forget the combination to the safe? Why did we doubt its power or misuse it? The answer is stress which, biologically, is fear. A brain chronically under stress is incapable of accessing the full measure of power that nature has bestowed. Neurologically, there is nothing more debilitating to brain function than a buildup of stress hormones from prolonged bouts of anxiety. What is the chief cause of stress? A fearful attitude. Dr. Bruce McEwen, the distinguished stress researcher, defined the problem poignantly in his book *The End of Stress as We Know It*: "No longer just a term used with pride to display the scars or medals of a fast paced life, 'stress' has come to mean fear for one's safety, health, and livelihood. It represents the loss of the assumption that the world is a safe place."[15]

We all go through episodes when stress gets the upper hand. We try to cope and reduce its impact, but the fact is every day we are losing ground. Stress is an epidemic. An annual survey conducted by the Gallup Organization reveals that stress is extreme for 40 percent of Americans and troublesome for another 40 percent.[16] Those working in education and health services appear to be hit hardest. Many of us believe we are doing a good job of coping with it until we take a closer look. The American Psychological Association, in its annual examination of stress in America, finds that most people underestimate their level of stress. Their studies show that while most people believe they are managing stress well, they also report that stress is having a negative impact on their physical and emotional well-being. Of the nearly two thousand people surveyed:

Three-quarters (77 percent) experienced physical symptoms during the last month as a result of stress. This includes fatigue (51 percent), headache (44 percent), upset stomach (34 percent), muscle tension (30 percent), change in appetite (23 percent), teeth grinding (17 percent), change in sex drive (15 percent), and feeling dizzy (13 percent), among others.

Nearly as many (73 percent) experienced psychological symptoms in the last month, including irritability or anger (50 percent), feeling nervous (45 percent), lack of energy (45 percent), and feeling fearful (36 percent).

Half (48 percent) of adults lay awake at night during the last month because of stress, and on average they report losing twenty-one hours of sleep per month.

Forty-three percent overeat or eat unhealthy foods, and more than one-third (36 percent) have skipped a meal because of stress during the last month.[17]

Clearly, most of America is not living the good life. But the problem is not limited to our shores. Studies reveal that the problem of stress is global.

THE STORM

Ordinary stress is the mind's bad weather that comes and goes, but chronic stress is tantamount to living at the edge of a gathering storm.

In that unstable condition, a disturbance as trivial as someone's offhand remark can generate a sense of threat, activating a part of our brain that treats every threat as if our life were on the line. Our mood darkens, thunder cracks, and memories of past traumas start to flash. If we mismanage the disturbance, which a brain chronically under stress is prone to do, our agitation can grow in intensity, building to a storm. Anxiety, anger, and overwhelm can become a whirl of flying debris that batters reason and compromises well-being. Attack and defense are sure to follow. Such experiences can crush the assertion that we are gifted with the most remarkable system in biology. Chronic stress is the system gone awry. It represents a brain in dissonance, toxic with stress hormones and incapable of higher intelligence.

> You taught me language, and my profit on't is,
> I know how to curse.
> **William Shakespeare**

Most people think it is not possible to transcend chronic stress. It is. To a mind under stress, this idea may appear hopelessly difficult, but it is simpler than we think. Most stress reactions are preventable. The first step in transcending stress is no longer finding value in the way stress makes us think, feel, or see the world. There are some people who believe stress does have value. When I define the problem of stress in my workshops, a participant invariably asserts that stress is good for motivating people and raising their level of performance.[18] It isn't. Chronic, repetitive bouts of stress actually produce the opposite effect.

Certainly, the biological mechanism known as the stress response system is good in specific situations but not in sustaining peak performance. A full-blown stress reaction in a real and present emergency can save one's life. Obviously, this is a critically important (and good) feature. There is also an element of this system called eustress. Hans Selye, the first scientist to demonstrate the existence of stress, coined the term. Eustress represents a sudden spike of arousal lasting for a few minutes at most. It is the thrill of riding a roller coaster or the internal alarm triggered by the bedside clock jolting us from sleep. It can be the rush of adrenaline we feel as we step to the podium or the simple excitement of a creative flash. It can also be the wave of fear that gets us focused on an approaching deadline. Eustress is meant to kick-start us. If the ride on the roller coaster suddenly speeds out of control, or if fear of failure freezes us at the podium, lower brain functions will intensify, depleting our energy and dulling higher mental activity. Robert Sapolsky of Stanford University sums it up well. The stress response system "is a wonderful adaptation should you come across a bear—but too much of a good thing and you're in trouble."[19]

We can break the vicious cycle of chronic stress for good. We can learn to direct our brain to deliver a stress-free mind to fulfill all that we are capable of fulfilling, personally and professionally.

WE CAN LEARN TO DIRECT OUR BRAIN TO DELIVER
A STRESS-FREE MIND SO WE CAN FULFILL
ALL THAT WE ARE CAPABLE OF FULFILLING.

THE EYE OF THE STORM

Moving from the storm of stress into the eye, where the mind is joyfully engaged and at peace, involves a simple but essential shift in attitude that anyone can make. When we sustain this shift, our brains begin to function as nature intended. Gamma wave activity, signaling higher mental acuity, steadily increases. Emotions begin working in harmony with reason rather than hijacking the mind. We activate neural circuitry to make us more loving and empathic, increasing interpersonal strength and facilitating an optimistic and constructive relationship with the world. Homeostasis locks in, securing the mind–body connection that generates optimal health. In short, we realize more of our innate potential to excel, to create fulfilling relationships, and to live a long and healthy life—all through a single but essential shift in attitude.

It is like catching three exotic birds with one net. I call it the neurocompetitive advantage.

The shift in attitude that locates the eye of the storm is the psychological shift from fear to peace. There is no greater gain in brain function and brain chemistry than this shift. Some think of peace as disengaging from the world, losing our edge and becoming passive and unmotivated. In actuality, peace is a dynamic state of being that generates neurological power. Peace is a fearless engagement with life that is the core condition for high performance, constructive relationships and greater well-being.

ATTITUDE IS NEUROPLASTIC; IT REWIRES THE BRAIN TO SUSTAIN THE EXPERIENCE A NEW ATTITUDE EVOKES.

Psychologist Mihaly Csikszentmihalyi of the University of Chicago conducted landmark research on human performance over decades. His research discovered a direct correlation between peak performance and a state of consciousness he called flow.[20] He found that this state of flow was present in rock climbers, dancers, chess players, athletes, artists, managers, farmers, fishermen, and housekeepers. In short, it was present in every form of human endeavor pursuing excellence. These best moments, as he called them, "usually occur when a person's body or mind is stretched to its limits in a voluntary effort to accomplish something difficult and worthwhile."[21] This sense of stretching ourselves is not experienced as stressful. A dynamically joyful, peaceful attitude generates a flow of experience that transcends effort, producing what Csikszentmihalyi referred to as "states of psychic negentrophy"[22] that flow freely into whatever challenge we undertake. In this state, results are predictably productive and generate an intrinsically rewarding experience of work and life. The polar opposite of flow is a "state of psychic entropy," which is produced by fear. In this state, we cannot use attention effectively to deal with external tasks and conditions. Psychic entropy is diminished mental capacity. It is the collapse of emotional stability and resilience. It is the body drained of physical energy. Psychic entropy is the brain under stress, incapable of sustaining the flow of peak performance.

MYSTIC COOL

Those who suffer in the storm often view those who have found the eye as genetically gifted, spiritually blessed, or just plain filthy rich. However, the optimal experience is alive in each of us, waiting for us to turn on the switch and set it in motion. It takes a fundamental shift in attitude to flip the switch. As we shall see, attitude is neuroplastic; it rewires the brain to sustain the experience a new attitude evokes. Eventually, the brain programs the experience to be second nature. It becomes a way of being that flows into whatever we are doing, enhancing the process at every level that matters. This stream of experience is what psychologists call flow, athletes call the zone, and mystics call effortless effort. This book calls it Mystic Cool, a concept that is fully presented in chapter 5. Mystic Cool is a practical approach to locating the eye of the storm.

PANTHEON OF THE BRAIN

The tangible result this book is seeking is peace and joy. It is the joy and peace we experience when using our inherent strengths and intelligence to pursue what is best in us so we can offer what we are here to contribute.

Sustaining a dynamically peaceful and joyful attitude involves persuading three parts of the brain to work together rather than against one another. Each of these parts of the brain represents a stage in the evolution of the human brain. Together they form a neurological pantheon of three gods, with a host of lesser gods that link all three into a functioning whole. The three gods of neurology are Apollo, or the neocortex; Mars, or the emotional brain; and Dragon, or the primitive brain.

These three gods of neurology are omnipotent and as wondrous as the gods of ancient cultures. They can also be as argumentative with one another and as troublesome as the gods of antiquity. Each has its own identifiable personality and talents that we often refer to as this or that side of ourselves. When the gods of neurology are in dissonance, the brain becomes a storm of dysfunction at the expense of intelligence.

When the gods of the brain work in harmony, we transcend personality and talent to reach the threshold of genius that is the mark of our species. As the great philosopher Arthur Schopenhauer put it: "Talent hits a target no one else can hit; genius hits a target no one else can see." When the gods are in harmony, the mind slips past the storm of stress and inner conflict, and walks out onto Elysian Fields to realize what Abraham Joshua Heschel called the "greatest miracle on Earth."

In the upcoming chapters, we will explore each of the three gods. Even a rudimentary understanding of the way each system works—and how each feels and behaves as it generates our experience—can help us in mapping our path to the eye.

**The difference between what we do
and what we are capable of doing would suffice
to solve most of the world's problems.**
Mahatma Gandhi

2
Dragon, The Primitive Brain

If not for the beast within us we would be castrated angels.

Hermann Hesse

The Dragon god of neurology, the oldest and smallest of the three parts of the brain, is the foundation from which the other two evolved. Often referred to as the primitive or reptilian brain, the Dragon is the body and is largely automatic, mindless body function under the command of the brain stem. But as we shall see, the primitive brain also endows the body with a mind of its own that is deep and rich in wisdom. It is our wild, animal nature that is attuned to Earth. The word *dragon* derives from the Greek word *drakein*, meaning "to see clearly." Seeing clearly is, in fact, a quality our primitive brain bestows.

In Greek myth, the dragon beast usually guarded a sacred spring, grove, or golden treasure. A dragon that never slept guarded the Golden Fleece in the sacred grove of Mars at Colchis. A pair of winged dragons drew the chariot of Demeter, the goddess of fertility, the guardian of youth, and the bringer of seasons, most notably the spring. These Greek myths place the dragon in front of the treasures that humanity reveres most, reminding us that we must pass through the primitive to get to the treasure. There is also the myth of Athena sowing dragon's teeth into the Earth to generate an army of full-grown, fully armed warriors. This represents the savage nature of the reptilian brain.

The Greeks were not the only culture with dragons. Native Americans revere the Dragon as the divine representative of all the primal forces in nature and the universe. In Eastern mythology the dragon is benevolent and in Western myths it is malevolent. Australian aboriginals call their reptilian god *Mangar-kunjer-kunja*, the god that created humans. The primitive brain is the good and evil out of which the human race springs.

THE MINDLESS BODY

The primitive brain is the mindless body. It controls the vegetative processes of the body, such as breathing, heartbeat, and digestion. If it fails to function, we die. It manages life support without generating a single thought, perception, or emotion. It is instinct, sex, and reflex. The primitive brain is the sole brain structure that we share with all of Earth's creatures: from animals to fish to insects.

Strictly speaking, a creature that possesses only the primitive brain is not thought to be intelligent. It appears to have no memory of its own experience. It does not seem to reason, compute, or choose its course. Rather, it is said to follow instinct. When we take a closer look, however, this mindless body appears to be smarter than we think. The more science studies animal behavior, the thinner the line becomes between instinct and intelligence. At times, pure instinct achieves and even exceeds results that intelligence produces. Birds, fish, and insects possessing only the primitive brain are able to navigate great distances across ocean or sky to return to a point of origin to spawn or retreat from winter. Bumble bees have an incredible homing instinct that allows them to find their way home from up to eight miles away. They are able to extract directional cues from Earth's magnetic fields, compute sky coordinates, and assess travel distance correctly.[1] Incredibly, bees are also able to communicate navigational coordinates to their brethren through precise movements of their tails, directing them to fields where flowers are in bloom. These coordinates actually factor in changes in the rotation of the Earth around the sun, accounting for the elapsed time since the bee was last in the field of flowers. The bumble bee knew, through its body, that the Earth was round and circled the sun, long before Copernicus figured it out.

In relying more and more on intellect, modern human beings have tended to repress primitive impulses, and not without reason. These impulses can get us into trouble. When the Dragon takes control of human behavior, it makes us highly territorial, concerned only with survival. It can also make us savage. When a platoon senselessly massacres defenseless people, it is probable that their minds, through fear, fatigue, and trauma, devolved brain function to the point that primitive instincts took control. Instinct kills to survive without giving it any thought. Clearly, we do not want our primitive nature in the Oval Office with its finger on the button. Reason is also leery of primitive passion, which is why mothers in most cultures chaperoned courtship for hundreds of years. It is why a father growls at a good-looking, hot-blooded boy with a fast car, who appears at the front door asking to see his daughter. In daily life, the primitive brain can also make us impulsive and precipitous. A conservative, properly regulated bank would not issue a credit card to our primitive nature. The intellect's need to impose some restraint is understandable. The rule of law, the penal code, and civility are Apollo's attempt to tame this wild beast. In taming the primitive, we moderns have come to think of this part of ourselves as crude and to view primitive cultures as undeveloped. We tend to dismiss messages from the primitive brain as too untrustworthy and unreliable to be intelligent.

THE BODY AS MIND

In truth, our body and mind have never been more attuned than when we were primitive, more in harmony with our immediate experience, more intelligent in our relationship to Earth, and more in touch with the sacred. We can recover enormous personal power by coaxing our rationality to listen with more respect to the information our primitive brain feeds us through the body. There is genius in it.

Mystic Cool

The movie *The Last of the Mohicans* offers a poignant representation of primitive power. In the opening scene, paraphrased here from the screenplay, we hear the forest, the call of some distant birds, and the sound of rustling getting closer and louder. Suddenly, a moccasined foot rockets through the frame. It is an Indian running hard, the sound of his breathing now heavy but even. He is a young man, tattooed, his head shaved bald. This is Uncas, the last of the Mohicans. In one hand he carries a flintlock musket. A calico shirt is gathered at the waist with a wampum belt of small white beads over a breechcloth. A long-handled tomahawk is stuffed in his belt.

The film cuts to another part of the forest, to another man running with a massive war club in his hand. He is heavier, older. Over his left eyebrow is the tattoo of a snake. This is Chingachgook, Uncas's godfather. He runs, disturbing no leaves, no branches, making no sound, running parallel to Uncas. They run through the cathedral of mature forest over streams, boulders and fallen trees, down into the ravine.

The film cuts to another part of the forest, to a man with long black hair, rocketing through trees. A long rifle is in his right fist. This is Nathaniel Poe, the white man the Iroquois have named Hawkeye. He flashes through the tree branches and then suddenly stops. We see the tan of an animal buried in the foliage two hundred and fifty yards away. Hawkeye raises the rifle to his shoulder. There is a loud click as his thumb cocks the lock holding the piece of flint. At the sound, Uncas and Chingachgook stop dead. Hawkeye shoots and the huge elk leaps at the sound into the .59 caliber round programmed to intercept him. Before gutting the beast, Chingachgook kneels on one knee and prays: *We are sorry to kill you, brother. Forgive us. I honor your courage and speed, and your strength.*[2]

This is an image of men who are at one with the environment, with each other, and with their goal to secure food for the survival of their people. It is as if the men, the land, and the animal are parts of one body traveling in one fluid movement through the only time that is forever here and now. The primitive brain is essentially outer-directed. It lives in the outer world, focuses the mind in the present moment, and uses the body to read and react to the world. Animals are primarily, if not exclusively, outer-directed, reacting instantly to visual, auditory, tactile, and environmental stimuli. In the wild, the primitive brain rivets attention on what is happening *out there.*

● ● ●

The creative, largely inner-directed mind that the higher brain generates is also apparent in the film's imagery. It is present in the technology the men carry. It is also present in their clothing; in the self-expression of their tattoos, shaved heads, and bead work; and in the prayer of thanksgiving that Chingachgook speaks over the fallen stag. Unlike animals, human beings are unique in that our brains are able to be outer- and inner-directed, both at the same time. Sensory information, gathered by the primitive brain through the body, is fed to another part of the brain where it is translated into the language of emotion. It is the part of us that sees, smells, hears, and registers what is happening at the moment and then determines how we feel about what we are sensing. Sensory and emotional data then passes through the higher brain and is integrated with prior information, memories, and knowledge. Sensing, feeling, and reasoning do not compete or conflict; they are attuned, generating resonance, as they did between the three warriors to produce the right behavior at the right time.

This is the way of the warrior. It is also the way of great leaders, who are able to bring coherence to their inner and outer experience. They are alert to the external situation; they read people's expressions and intonations, and sense the atmosphere in the room. They feel the emotional resonance or dissonance that is present. They interpret their own emotional reaction accurately and manage it well. When it all comes together, like a lens reaching focus, they articulate a response that helps makes sense of the immediate situation within a larger context. It is the same integrated way of being that makes a great teacher, coach, or parent. It is what makes a trader successful on the floor of the stock market. It is what makes a marriage flourish.

It is arguable that modern human beings—in the way we walk the Earth—are not as integrated and therefore not as alive as our ancestors.

We tend to be much more inner-directed. We are much less attuned to the Earth and are often out of touch with our immediate physical experience. As a result, we are less adept at translating the language of the body into action. It is also arguable that our ancestors had better brains than we do. Science has found that physical exertion actually creates a neurological condition called "enriched environment."[3] The wilderness pushed our ancestors to do more physically, and brains respond to physical exertion by generating more nerve cells to build a bigger brain. The brain uses these new cells to thicken the cortex, strengthen synapses, and sprout more branches, so we can live up to our potential. A developed brain was necessary in the wilderness. A lot of brain structure is required to produce the kinetic intelligence and mental toughness to run down an elk.

There are times when it seems we moderns do not even want to be in our body. We are much more inner-directed, tending to rely more on our heads than our hearts, more on logic and rationality than intuition, more on figuring things out than feeling our way. We lead highly structured lives that have exchanged spontaneity for predictability. It can cause a human being to lose touch with concrete reality and become ungrounded. We tend to live our lives less in the moment, less in our direct experience, and more and more in our thinking, unable to decipher feeling states generated by the body. It can make us indecisive, pedantic, one-dimensional, and even crazy. At times, we can feel alienated from the outside world, without a sense of who we are and why we are here.

The fact that human beings have graduated from the wild does not mean we have lost the capacity for a more integrated way of being. A walk in nature is enough to revive the strong mind and heart of our ancestors—if we walk with awareness. All it takes is quieting our mind; following our breathing; feeling the ground beneath us, the wind on our skin; hearing the birds, the rustle of trees and water; and watching the insects as we skim our fingertips over the tall grass. At some point, inside and outside begin to merge. Body and mind begin to entwine like lovers. Our troubles start to dissolve into a natural order of things.

Our mind surrenders the need to figure out any particular problem and starts to feel its way to a deeper understanding of life. It is the process through which the receptive becomes creative, hearing becomes listening, sensing becomes sensitivity, seeing becomes understanding, understanding becomes compassion, and together it all becomes love. We may even begin to feel the spontaneity of our wild heart awaken, willing to take a chance on something new that could change our life.

The Mohicans, Hopi, Sioux, Huichols, and other—if not all—indigenous cultures have long understood how our primitive nature works in harmony with our higher mind to generate an intelligence that, at times, feels mystical. It springs from an inner grandeur penetrating the natural grandeur that surrounds us. Albert Einstein also understood this: "The most beautiful and profound emotion we can experience," he wrote, "is the sensation of the mystical. It is the sower of all true science." It seems clear that the primitive brain is at the bottom of that experience. Neuroscience is beginning to find evidence for it. "Primitive brain structures," stated Earl K. Miller, the preeminent cognitive neuroscientist at MIT, "might be the engine driving even our most advanced high-level, intelligent learning abilities."[4]

GUT FEELING INTELLIGENCE

Intuition is one of the essential forms of intelligence that the three gods of neurology create together. Neurologically, intuition is information that emanates from the body and travels up to the prefrontal cortex. The prefrontal cortex is a crucial part of higher brain function and the point where the primitive brain, the emotional brain, and the neocortex converge. In one fluid motion, we register a sensation in our gut, internally feel and interpret what we sense, correlate what it tells us with what we know from memory, filter our possible choices through moral values, and then act from what feels right.

"Feelings offer us a glimpse of what goes on in our flesh," wrote Dr. Antonio Damasio.[5] In his theory on somatic states, Damasio proposes that the brain's ability to monitor sensations arising from the gut is crucial to what is called adaptive decision making. Neurons in the gut appear to signal impending danger, risk, or punishment, or the opposite—the expectation of reward. Intuition is particularly useful when a decision must be made quickly in a situation where uncertainty is present. It is the feeling that decides for an executive in the absence of data. It is what induces a trader to bet against the odds. It is the read that allows a woman to trust a suitor's intentions, and a police officer to sense when someone is lying, underhanded, or potentially harmful. It is the same with a mother who knows her child inside out, detecting the slightest change in tone, mood, or body language. It is the poet who intuits the exact line or word that unifies the poem. It is also a physician who sees through complex and sometimes disparate facts to diagnose an illness.

We call it gut feeling, and those who have cultivated the noetic art of listening to their intuition acquire wisdom that the intellect alone cannot reach. Some of the biggest mistakes we make in life are the result of ignoring a gut feeling. The gut is also the place where we find or lose courage, where the thrill of a win is felt, as when a basketball player sinks a shot, and the place where the pain of defeat registers when the shot misses.

THE INTELLIGENCE OF THE HEART

Another part of the Dragon that contributes a rich and unique form of intelligence is the heart. "The idea that we can think with our hearts," stated Joseph Chilton Pearce, "is no longer just a metaphor, but is, in fact, a very real phenomenon."[6] The heart, like the gut, possesses its own brain structure. It contains a large number of nerve cells, identical to those in the brain. Half of these neurons appear to be dedicated to establishing a direct neural connection with the emotional brain, keeping both in constant communication and enabling us to feel, express, and act on our emotions.[7] "The emotional brain makes a qualitative evaluation of our experience of this world," stated Pearce, "and sends that information instant-by-instant down to the heart. In return, the heart exhorts the brain to make the appropriate response."[8] Rarely do we think of an open heart as the means to gathering information that increases intelligence.

Unfortunately, the heart is not always successful in mediating an appropriate response. When Mars, or the emotional brain, senses a threat and reactively takes command, the siege that follows can quake the heart with fear. Fear generates a dissonant pattern of neural signals traveling from the heart to the brain, which appears to inhibit higher cognitive functions. This limits our ability to think clearly, remember, learn, reason, and make effective decisions. Emotionally, we feel the dissonance as discouragement, or what we colloquially refer to as losing heart. Conversely, positive emotional states enhance brain function.[9] When we sustain feelings of love, respect, or appreciation, our blood pressure, respiration, and other oscillating systems entrain to the heart's rhythm and synchronize with the rhythms of the brain. It is a state of resonance, restoring the cognitive and emotional intelligence that a dissonant pattern of fear blocks.

FORESIGHT

Foresight is another powerful gift that the heart bestows on human beings. A number of studies suggest that the heart is involved in what we generally think of as premonition.[10] The terms science uses to describe this ability are *prestimulus response* and *nonlocality*. Nonlocality means that the heart and brain receive and respond to information about a future event before the event actually happens.[11] We all have premonitions from time to time. The phone rings and we instantly know who it will be, even when we have been out of contact with this person. We marvel at the foresight of great artists, inventors, mystics, and social visionaries, who are so often ahead of their times. Entrepreneurs like Steve Jobs and Bill Gates, artists like Pablo Picasso and Bob Dylan, and social reformers like Mahatma Gandhi and Theodore Roosevelt all possess this ability. They demonstrate a kind of cultural prescience, through which they see a future that, a generation or two later, society actually reaches. These visionaries access a wider range of information from a fuller use of all their inner resources. They are open to experiences most of us miss. It may be that this quality of openness wires their brains to produce a kind of sixth sense, enabling them to see deeper into the collective psyche and farther down the road on which the times are traveling. Jesus said to the Pharisees: "You know how to interpret the appearance of the sky, yet you can't interpret the signs of the times?"[12] It would seem the Pharisees could not recognize the future Jesus represented because their hearts were closed. Neurologically, it may be that their closed hearts blocked their capacity for foresight.

THE NONCONCEPTUAL SELF: OUR INNER VOICE

"We should take care not to make the intellect our god," Albert Einstein warned. "It has, of course, powerful muscles, but no personality. It cannot lead; it can only serve." We are often seduced into isolating ourselves in the abstract world of the mental. "Being aware of the input of our body, especially information from the neural networks surrounding intestines and heart, enables us to be open to the wisdom of our nonconceptual selves."[13]

Our culture tends to define *self* in a highly conceptual manner, in terms of our roles, jobs, and social status, as well as past failures and successes, and future goals. These have their place, but they can also calcify. Our sense of self can become a strategic plan in which we market an artificial exterior to the world, in hopes the world will accept it and thus establish our authenticity. The discovery that this approach does not yield a genuine experience of self is often the first step in self-discovery. We possess a deeper nature, from which the whole of our being emerges, rendering a greater life experience and generating a more powerful effect in the world—an effect that the conceptual self can never attain. Mercifully, reaching our deeper nature could not be simpler. It is accessed through openness to our experience, moment to moment. It is attuning our attention to body, mind, and soul, listening to the information it offers.

"The fully functioning person," wrote Carl R. Rogers, the father of humanistic psychology, "makes use of all of the information his nervous system can thus supply, using it in awareness but recognizing that his total organism may be, and often is, wiser than his awareness."[14] There is a classic archetype in literature that illustrates what it means to live from our total organism. It is the likes of Shakespeare's Falstaff, and Nikos Kazantzakis' Zorba the Greek. They are giant literary forms that represent the development of a fully actualized human being from the primal ground up. This earthy character is generally portrayed as a sidekick to a man of privilege with limited life experience. The tightly wrapped protagonist is subsequently pulled into adventures and calamities by his more spontaneous, spirited companion and, through the process, is lifted to a more authentic life. In a similar way, the primitive brain augments intellect and emotion with heart and gut instinct to make a whole human being.

We love these sidekicks because they are completely honest and unpretentious, which makes them more human. They are real flesh and blood, full of passion, physical vitality, and daring, and as imperfect as the rest of us. They teach us how to embrace life by embracing this moment, here and now. In them, we recognize the genius spawned from boldness. We see the rewards derived from taking risks and come to understand that wisdom is our greatest gain, attained through the trial and error of living life fully and openly. They also teach us to laugh at life, especially at ourselves and the stupidities our daring sometimes commits. They embody the light and dark side of our wild nature, becoming conscious through the choice to love. As a result, they teach us to see more than we have been willing to see, feel more than we have been willing to feel, and learn more than we know.

This archetype represents the primitive becoming sentient, the sentient reaching back to the primitive to realize the essence of human nature, which is free. French Philosopher Jean-Jacques Rousseau said, "Man is born free, but everywhere he is in chains."[15] Rousseau was referring to political repression, but great literary artists take us a step deeper, to elucidate the chains of our own restrictive ego. In placing this wild sage in juxtaposition to a constricted person of privilege, literature paints us a picture of how bound and constricted the conceptualized self becomes, and how alive the individuated self becomes when the chains are removed.

No other novel has articulated this archetype better than Nikos Kazantzakis' masterpiece *Zorba the Greek*. What makes Zorba even more compelling as a figure is the fact that he was a real person; he is actually one of us. His name was Georgis Zorbas, and he was a lifelong friend of the author. I had the opportunity to meet Kazantzakis' wife, Helen, and she told me Anthony Quinn's portrayal of Zorba in the award-winning movie captured the essence and personality of

the Zorba she knew and loved. Zorba possessed, in the words of Nikos Kazantzakis, the "primordial glance . . . the creative alertness, renewed each morning, which enabled him to see all things constantly as though for the first time." Zorba had "the gallant daring to tease the soul, as though inside him he had a force superior to the soul." He would point to sea birds and say, "that's the road to take; find the absolute rhythm and follow it with absolute trust." He possessed a "savage bubbling laugh that was able to demolish the barriers that hobble a life . . . Even the most insignificant incidents connected with Zorba," Kazantzakis wrote in his autobiography, "gleamed with clarity, were quick-moving and precious like colorful fish in a transparent ocean."[16]

"What's happening today, this minute," Zorba said, "that's what I care about." "True happiness," he said, "[is] to have no ambition and to work like a horse as if you had every ambition. [It is] to live far from men, not to need them and yet to love them; it is being wherever you are, and not let it scare you."[17] These statements, reduced to traits, describe, in part, the nature of our primitive brain. Even his idea of God was primitive. "Let's go outside," he would say when he needed to pray, "where God can see us better."

Like Einstein, Zorba warned against making a god of the intellect. "You think too much," he said to his pedantic friend. "That is your trouble. Clever people and grocers, they weigh everything. Come on, friend, make up your mind. Take the plunge. A man needs a little madness ... or else ... he never dares cut the rope and be free." It is the challenge to cut the rope to the conceptual self and take the plunge, which is how an embodied mind feels when it lets go of fear. It resonates with the aliveness of daring. "If I had listened to his voice," Kazantzakis wrote, "my life would have had more value. I would have experience with blood, sweat, and bone what I now ponder like a hashish-smoker."[18]

This deeper primal nature exists in each person, and it calls to us. It appears to know, with clarity, who and what we really are. It knows where we want to go, how to get there, and what we are here to realize and contribute. This deeper nature emerges when gut, heart, and head unite to generate an exponential intelligence. As we will see, we have the capacity to wire our brain to attain this integration. Insight, foresight, and intuition can wire together to form an inner voice that speaks to us and guides us. At times, this inner voice points us to the edge of a new world and entreats us to take a leap of faith. Other times, it pulls us back from the edge of disaster. Without this inner guide, there is no real and personal sense of odyssey. We are left with only our conceptual self, which is often a façade or an anxious insecurity seeking approval by conforming to the expectations of others.

Steve Jobs, in his commencement address to Stanford graduates in 2005, counseled: "Don't let the noise of others' opinions drown out your own inner voice.... Have the courage to follow your heart and intuition. They somehow already know what you truly want to become. Everything else is secondary."[19] Kazantzakis and Jobs may not have been aware of it, but what they point toward is not merely inspirational; it is neurological power.

3

Apollo, The Neocortex

We lie in the lap of immense intelligence.

Ralph Waldo Emerson

Apollo, the second god of neurology, epitomizes the power of the neocortex. This is the last part of the brain to evolve. The neocortex is often viewed as intellect, but like Apollo, its dominion extends beyond mere intellect. Apollo represents the conscious mind reaching mastery in the physical, emotional, and intellectual realms, which is why ancient Greeks regarded him as the most important of the Olympian gods. One of the great masterpieces of Greek sculpture is *Apollo of Anzio*. The Romans admired this statue so much that they copied it. The face is eternally youthful and looks straight at us with a gentle, open expression of noetic calm. It is difficult to tell if the statue is a man or a woman. In whatever way you look at it, it has a magnificent face. Its masculine and feminine principles appear to be in perfect balance, as is true in the creative process. Creative intelligence is the very essence of Apollo and the neocortex. The masculine and feminine principles merge within the neocortex to generate our capacity for maternal love and empathy along with our ability to analyze and make decisions.

Apollo is the part of the brain that lifted humans to the top of the food chain. The Greeks viewed Apollo as prophetic, with the ability to direct the future, bending the world to his will. He had dominion over civil affairs, tamed the beast to serve man, governed science, and ruled the arts. He was the leader of the Muses and the director of their choir. When Apollo directs the choir in our brain, the brain becomes a harmony of intellect, emotion, and sensation to produce a fully integrated, fully functioning human being

THE COURT OF APOLLO: THE PREFRONTAL CORTEX

The land Apollo governs is the neocortex. Apollo's court is housed in a part of the neocortex called the prefrontal cortex. It is the only area of the brain where all three gods of the triune sit in council. It is Apollo's job to keep the peace and bring about harmony. Mars—the emotional brain—can make peace-keeping difficult, which is why Mars was disliked by the other gods of classical mythology. But there is much good that comes from the alliance of Apollo and Mars. In linking with Mars, Apollo morphs the primal emotion of fear into feelings as deep, rich, and varied as love.

From his throne in the prefrontal cortex, Apollo performs a number of executive functions, from setting goals to making plans for achieving his goals to executing those plans. He generates the working memory that focuses our attention on the here and now as well as abstracting models to predict and ultimately shape the future. He is able to multitask multiple goals, detect and correct errors, adapt to change, and maintain focus on the big picture. He is the quintessential chief executive.

In addition, Apollo's court (the prefrontal cortex) is home to the better angels of our nature.[1] It is the foundation for everything we think of as a fully integrated and fully functioning person. It makes what we call a good human being. In *The Mindful Brain*, Daniel Siegel, MD, described these better angels. There are nine in all:

1. Body regulation is controlled, coordinating and balancing the sympathetic (accelerator) and parasympathetic (brakes) branches of the autonomic nervous system. This allows us to energetically engage or calmly disengage from situations.

2. Attuned communication is achieved, enabling us to tune into another's state of mind to establish interpersonal resonance.

3. Emotional balance is maintained, permitting us to become aroused enough so life feels vibrant and meaningful, but not so aroused that we become manic, chaotic, or overwhelmed with emotion.

4. Response flexibility is reached, which is the opposite of a knee-jerk reaction. This capacity enables us to pause before acting and inhibit impulses, giving us enough time to reflect on our various options for response.

5. Empathy is invoked, allowing us to consider the mental perspective of another person: to see, feel, and understand a situation from someone else's point of view.

6. Insight is acquired through input and output fibers to parts of the brain that produce representations of autobiographical memories with emotional texture, linking past, present, and future to form our life story.

7. Fear-related behavior is attenuated through the stimulation of inhibitory $GABA_A$ receptors, suggesting that growth of these fibers reverses the fear conditioning causing chronic stress.

8. Intuition is generated through information from the neural networks surrounding our intestines (gut feelings) and our heart (heartfelt feelings), enabling us to be open to the wisdom of our nonconceptual selves.

9. Morality is established, fostering the capacity to transcend a limited self-interest and think for the larger good, to imagine what is best for the whole.

Each of these functions expresses an attribute of inner peace. The neural integration[2] of all these functions creates a dynamically peaceful human being, with the ability to connect and live with purpose. Most of us think of these nine functions, not as inborn neurological properties, but as virtues drilled into us by our moral superiors. When I was growing up, Sister Bernadette enforced some of these with her ruler. But these qualities are embedded; they are domains that are part of the operating system we were born with. They do not need to be beat into us. They can be trusted to emerge naturally when we remove the condition of fear that blocks their full expression.

Ironically, the potential for a dynamically peaceful human being, wired for higher consciousness, is standing along side the potential for an inherently fearful human being, wired for fight-or-flight. Our brain is wired for both. The brain has evolved deep neuro-circuits of fear as well as peace. Evolution also built brain structure to choose between the two. A difficult childhood or an unfortunate expression of genes may have initially wired us for fear, but at some point most of us turn and face our life and ask, is this the life I want. It invariably comes down to a choice between fear and peace. Given that four of the nine prefrontal functions boost the other five by quelling fear, it appears that evolution is supporting the choice for peace. In making adaptations, evolutions always puts survival first, and it seems evolution understood before we did that our survival as a species would ultimately depend on the full expression of our peaceful nature. Personal happiness and success depends on it as well, which suggests that evolution also wanted us to be happy and to succeed.

The choice for peace is attained by letting go of fear, which requires mindfulness. By mindfulness I am referring to an openness and acceptance of our immediate experience. The more we can open to our experience, moment to moment, the more aware we will be of the fear conditioning that blocks the better angles of our nature. Remaining open allows us to see the painful illusions that fear generates and experience how easily illusions dissolve when we don't believe them.

As we change, our brain changes, integrating all nine of the prefrontal functions. Cultivating an open and receptive state of mind has been shown to increase cortical thickness and even preserve neural tissue through the aging process.[3] "With a receptive mind," Siegel stated, "it may be that this vertical integration naturally occurs ... [transforming] a disconnected way of living into a richer, more integrated way of living." When Alexander the Great visited Diogenes and asked whether he could do anything for the famed teacher, Diogenes replied: "Only stand out of my light." We have to stand out of our own neural light by letting go of fear. It is how intelligence grows into wisdom.

HOW INTELLIGENT DOES PEACE MAKE US?

How intelligent does peace make us? The answer is: far more so than we realize. Peace, as neurology is beginning to view it, is higher brain function providing emotional, social, and creative intelligence that sometimes opens to the transcendental experience Einstein called the sensation of the mystical.

Most of us do not give peace the chance to show us what it can do. In our drive to succeed, we often make achievement harder than it needs to be. The power of a dynamically peaceful attitude to achieve neocortical power springs from an easy, fluid quality of presence, quietly engaging the challenge at hand, becoming fully present in the moment, and effectively sweeping aside all outside distractions. It is attention to the step we are taking, constantly attuning our mind to the changing landscape of experience. In this state of mind, we are able to zero in on what is essential and discard the tangential. Our preoccupation with past and future disappears, and we seem to lose track of time and space. As the mind calms and gradually reaches clarity, it produces a flow of experience that makes work effortless. The usual internal tumult of self-doubt and self-concern disappear, giving way to a fearless self-confidence. We reach a kind of productive harmony, where we are using our skills to the fullest, engendering positive feelings of freedom, enjoyment, fulfillment, and competence. This is intelligence at its absolute best. Everything we have learned from books, experience, and association is accessible. All the skill we have developed through repetition now effortlessly comes into play. The various models we have imagined for how this or that might work best suddenly distill into the one that actually does.

Even though our work is reaching for an outcome, achieving the end result becomes secondary to the experience we are having. At the end of working in this way, we realize that the experience was the reward. This is not to say that what we achieve in tangible terms is insignificant. What we produce at these times often astounds us as well as others.

This experience is the antithesis of the proverbial putting our nose to the grindstone. We emerge from a day guided by Apollo with a stronger sense of self than when we began. At the end of the day, our energy is intact and our mind feels wide open. On the drive home from work, we find ourselves appreciating the beauty of the way daylight filters through dusk, gradually becoming night. If we stop at the grocery store, we notice in ourselves a friendlier attitude toward other shoppers. Coming through the front door to rejoin our families, we feel we have more to give emotionally than we do on other evenings.

THE GIFT CALLED FLOW

This is the experience of flow, discussed in chapter 1. Flow is the Apollo of our being stepping forward to meet a challenge, pulling on Mars for emotional power and the Dragon for heart, energy, and intuitive insight to generate the joy, focus, and purpose that excels. If we have, on the other hand, had a run of highly stressful days, this experience can seem like a pipe dream. It is not a pipe dream. We are capable of reaching an optimal state when attention, motivation, and a task that stretches our abilities all come together. It is the zone athletes depend on, artists summon, and intellectuals stumble into. Andrew Cooper's *Playing In the Zone* gives us a vivid picture of the zone through the eyes of athletes:

> In his autobiography, My Life and the Beautiful Game, *soccer star Pelé recalls a day when he experienced a strange calmness. "It was a type of euphoria," he wrote. "I felt I could run all day without tiring. I felt I could dribble through any of their team or all of them. I felt as if I could almost pass through them physically." For Michael Jordan, "The rim seems like a big ol' huge bucket." According to Golden State Warriors' John Starks, "It's like you see something just before it really happens." John Olerud of baseball's New York Mets says, "When things are going well, there seems to be more time to react to a pitch. And it doesn't matter what that pitch is."*[4]

Science is no stranger to the zone. Nineteenth-century chemist Dmitri Mendeleyev, taking a break from his labors, fell into a daydream while chamber music played in an adjacent room. In this altered state, he had the insight that basic chemical elements are in relationship with one another, comparable to phrases in music. From this sudden vision, he was able to write out the entire periodic table, the basis of modern chemistry. Friedrich Kekulé, a German chemist of the same era, fell into a reverie and understood the nature of the motion of atoms. He spent the remainder of the night sketching on paper what he had seen during his reverie. It was the origin of the structural theory of molecules. Einstein is even rumored to have said that conceptualizing the theory of special relativity was almost easy.

Art is replete with similar experiences. Paul McCartney of the Beatles penned the classic ballad *Yesterday* in the same way. "I woke up with a lovely tune in my head," McCartney recalled. He went to the piano and began working with the melody that—thirty-five years later—music experts would vote the best pop song of the 20th century. Flow can arise from carefully listening to one's experience. Melanesian sailors can be taken blindfolded to points of the ocean within a radius of several hundred miles of their island home. If allowed to float for a few minutes, the men are able to pinpoint the location.[5]

The zone is a moment of truth when a clear mind fuses with the wild heart that assumes there is nothing our total organism cannot do. The synergy of the two generates a lucid vision through which we see the quest realized. The vision then propels us forward to turn the image into reality. The zone is not really about outcomes of winning or losing, succeeding or failing. It is about the joy of stretching beyond our limits. Every person who has attained greatness did so by penetrating the joy at the core of the zone.

THE NEOCORTEX

We are never more intelligent than at those moments when we locate the zone. Ralph Waldo Emerson seems to have stated this fact when he wrote: "We lie in the lap of immense intelligence, which makes us receivers of its truth and organs of its activity."[6] The organ that makes us receivers of its truth is the neocortex. Whereas the prefrontal cortex gifts us with wholeness, the neocortex gifts us with genius. The neocortex has been described as more complex than the weather and more mysterious than a supernova. These poetic images illuminate the fact that the neocortex is a powerful force of nature, not to be dismissed.

The neocortex currently rules our planet. This force sits inside each of us, its immense power at our disposal for good or ill. Almost everything we define as intelligence—perception, language, imagination, mathematics, commerce, art, music, and strategic thinking—occurs in the neocortex.[7] Jeff Hawkins, author of *On Intelligence* and the man who invented the PalmPilot, says even though basic computers process operations at a rate five million times faster than the neocortex, the neocortex is much faster at completing the task. How? The neocortex never takes more than a hundred steps to finish the job, whereas a battery of a high-end computer requires billions or trillions of steps. In other words, basic computers may sprint faster, but they have infinitely farther to go to cross the finish line. "The largest conceivable parallel computer can't do anything useful in one hundred steps," Hawkins wrote, "no matter how large or fast."[8] The neocortex, on the other hand, can change the world in less than a hundred steps; and it has.

Currently two ambitious projects are underway in an attempt to create artificial intelligence, using the brain as a model. The hope is to perfect a twenty-billion neuron simulation of the human cortex and its peripheral systems on a cluster of five hundred computers. If successful, it will be the largest computer in history. However, most of the tasks the neocortex performs will still be beyond the capacity of this or any other computer. When the engineers work on models for artificial intelligence, the neocortex is doing the work, and even it cannot plumb its own depths or decode its own intricate patterns and algorithms. The odd thing is: the neocortex is actually much smaller than the smallest laptop computer. It is about as long and as wide as the book you are holding but much, much thinner. It is no thicker than two credit cards, one on top of the other.

Despite its size, the inside of the neocortex is immeasurable, bordering on infinite. Packed into its limited space are thirty billion nerve cells, or three times the number of stars in the Milky Way. The number of synapses providing the connection between these cells is larger than science can count, ranging from thirty to one hundred fifty trillion. The neocortex is a dynamo that never shuts down. It is open for business 24/7, including religious holidays. Its neurons fire from one to a hundred times a second, and most of its synapses are constantly flickering from one to fifty times a second. It is like a room filled with fireflies.

It is interesting that this remarkable gift of biology, providing our five senses, our emotions, our motor skills, and the vast intelligence to light our way, works entirely in the dark, makes no sound, and cannot feel. But it managed to see the path that took us from the bottom of the food chain to the top. The neocortex has an incredible capacity to learn and adapt to thousands of situations and environments, even those about which it previously had no knowledge or experience.

In evolution, adaptability means survival. Up to this point, our survival as a species has been secured by the neocortex. It removed the threat we faced in the jungle. Ironically, most of the threats we now face as a species derive from the scientific and technological progress we have made by applying the neocortex. In mythology, Apollo is also the bringer of plagues and disease. If we dodge our own bullet, it will be the prefrontal cortex that expands our consciousness to relate globally and the neocortex that stretches our ingenuity to clean up the mess it made.

Evolution is an ascent towards consciousness.
P. Teilhard de Chardin

AH-HA

If the neocortex has a signature emotion it is *ah-ha*. The neocortex is holographic in the way it works toward solutions. It does not need the full picture to see the whole. It is constantly filling in what is missing, like the neighbor's legs blocked from view by the hedge, or the way logic instantly fills in the part of a sentence our hearing missed. It is how our fingertips can identify an object we cannot see. When we cross a fast-flowing stream, the neocortex processes what it sees, filling in by inference what it can't see—the width of the stream, the water's depth, how fast the stream is flowing. To these data it adds what it knows about streams, its assessment of our agility, the odds of our making it across, and the consequences of slipping or falling. It creates a visual picture or model of how to cross the stream and compares it with memories of past experience. Each consideration is a neuron responding to a particular variable in the process of decision making. If we decide to cross the stream, the neocortex guides the body in approximation to the model it made. We would be hard-pressed to articulate every variable of thought, feeling, and deduction we considered in arriving at our decision. The algorithm the neocortex used to make even this small decision is simply too vast and too fast for us to recount.[9] As we cross the stream, the neocortex delicately manages to coordinate the sensory and somatic processes that carry our body across.

It is much the same with intellectual processes. We imagine a rough picture or model of what we hope to accomplish and then pursue it step by step. From memory, we make predictions. We associate the past with present to predict the future. The more we predict the correct answer, the more intelligent we are said to be. Of course, we are never working on just one model. We have a list of models representing a host of problems we want to solve and plans we want to bring to fruition. Neurons form to hold each item along with the data we collect as part of our fact finding. We work and work on the problem and then one day all the pieces of the puzzle fall into place, sometimes just as we are about to throw in the towel. Suddenly everything fits magnificently. We have our answer. We tend to think of these ah-ha moments as flashes of insight or even divine intervention. These sudden moments of illumination may be explained as the neurons, holding pieces of information, suddenly reaching consensus. There also may be neurons holding pieces of relevant information stored in our brain long ago, seemingly forgotten, that now suddenly awaken to add a key piece. "That's *it!*" the chorus of participating neurons announces, stimulating a joyful vibration that resonates through us. It may even be that a neuron holding a seemingly unrelated fact serves as the lens for the flash of neural light that projects the hologram we see as our solution. Some of science's great mysteries have been solved just so.

The way each neocortex is wired is as individual as our fingerprints. It makes me, me; and you, you. It also has an incredibly large memory capacity, enough to store everything we learn in a lifetime. In these cells are stored our knowledge, skills, abilities, dreams, and most of our memories. The neocortex takes all these pieces and configures our sense of self.

OUR GENIUS DAWNED ON US, SUDDEN-LIKE

Although human beings have possessed the neocortex for at least one hundred thirty thousand years, the paleoanthropologic record indicates that we did not tap its full potential for the first eighty thousand years.[10] No one knows why. Then suddenly, about fifty thousand years ago, the neocortex kicked in with a surge of ingenuity, lifting our species to the top of the food chain and eventually to world supremacy through migration. The neocortex made migration possible by enabling us to adapt to new climates and environments. It fitted us with the proper clothing and shoes, crafted warm and ventilated huts, and exploited the bounty with sophisticated tools and weapons. About eleven thousand years ago, the neocortex decoded the cycle of life, masterminding agriculture, inventing the plow, and coaxing the beast to live within our fences. It transformed survival into safety through family and community, and six thousand years ago it began establishing cities. It learned to cure diseases with plants, to stitch wounds, to mend broken bones, and eventually to perform surgery, transforming tools that were first developed to take lives into tools to save lives. Art, science, commerce, and democracy flourished, and philosophies arose to explain who we are in relation to all that is.

THE DORDOGNE VALLEY: THE ASCENT OF MAN

I once spent a week in the Dordogne Valley in France, one of the great archaeological wonders of the world. As I drove into town, I passed a team of paleontologists digging in the ground, looking for clues to the origins of humanity. The remains of nearly every stage of human development have been found in this valley. On exhibit in the valley floor are the soot-covered caves of a small band of Neanderthals, who lived just

across the river from the site where a handful of Homo sapiens had settled. Sixty thousand years ago, each species, faced with extinction from massive droughts in Africa caused by climate change, separately made their way out of Africa to this place. Incredibly, at that time, the number of Homo sapiens on the planet had shrunk to less than 2,000 people.[11] Half of that number traveled north, trekking across arid African savannahs and deserts into the bitter cold landscape of Europe. A small splinter group settled in the Dordogne and made a last stand for the human race. Neanderthals eventually disappeared, but our ancestors flourished. They created the first art we know of, painting bison and deer on cave walls. They discovered the principles of farming, learned to build with rock, and eventually erected castles on hillsides along the run of the river. Today, the quaint little village where I dined on wonderful French cuisine is surrounded by a patchwork quilt of farms. Adjacent to the town square is a museum of Impressionist art and a Romanesque church. All the houses of the village are made of stone, expertly fitted together, still standing after one hundred or more years, constructed to be both practical and elegant. There is also a hotel that caters to the affluent, people who come in hi-tech, luxury automobiles to spend their holiday. It is awe-inspiring to ponder how far our species has come.

The Dordogne is a magnificent monument of the climb the neocortex has made, through trial and error, as it developed the mastery that would eventually decode genetics, split the atom, map the brain, and take us to the moon and back. The neocortex's capacity for genius is personified throughout history, from Mozart to Beethoven, Copernicus to Einstein, Shakespeare to Picasso, Lincoln to Mandela, DiMaggio to Ali, and Mohammed to Rumi. The feats of each of these people were not entirely or even largely individual. We all stand on the shoulders of giants, which is the pinnacle one of us reaches through the accomplishments of many. The story of human history is like a cathedral built stone by stone, carried and set in place by far too many hands for history to record. Instead, history represents each stone with the name of a person whose head stood above the crowd. In a very real sense, however, these feats belong to the whole of humanity, which means they belong to you and me as much as to Einstein and Shakespeare. Each of our lives carries a stone right now, one that is our small contribution to the wing each generation adds to the cathedral that all of humanity has built and is building. The spirit of legacy that is a covenant of humanity is captured in the lyrics of Gene Scheer: "Each generation from the plains to distant shores, with the gifts that they were given were determined to leave more."[12]

THE TROUBLE

"If all this is true about human beings," a friend asked me once on a walk down the promenade along Waikiki Beach, "why do we get into so much trouble?" It is a question on most of our minds. Albert Camus, the great French writer, who fought for the French Resistance during World War II, alludes to the daunting crisis that is part of the human legacy. In his acceptance speech for the Nobel Prize, he stated, "Each generation doubtless feels called upon to reform the world. Mine knows that it will not reform it, but its task is perhaps even greater. It consists in preventing the world from destroying itself." The trouble both my friend and Camus were referring to is also evident in the Dordogne Valley, in the village of Oradour-sur-Glane. The village is a paradigm of human brutality, still as the Nazis left it after massacring men, women, and children, and burning the village to the ground.

What makes Adolf Hitler, Joseph Stalin, Radovan Karadzic, and Charles Manson? What turns a mother into the proverbial Mommy Dearest? What produces the leadership that generates a corporate culture so intensely competitive that it becomes immoral and even criminal, as it did in the financial sector in 2008? Barbara Oakley, in her book *Evil Genes*, suggests part of the reason may be faulty wiring. Poor genetics may produce an unfortunate neurological arrangement that psychological traumas can exacerbate. The area of the brain that appears to be involved is the amygdala, the brain's fear center—core to

Mars, or the emotional brain. It is possible that in these people the neural fibers that run from the prefrontal cortex to the fear center are too thin to extinguish destructive emotions. Empathy, attuned communication, emotional balance, and especially morality may fail to develop normally, leading to an absence of conscience. The result can be a malignantly narcissistic, nightmarish personality. Malignant narcissists can be quite seductive. They often possess a charismatic charm that camouflages their Machiavellian core, even to themselves. They see themselves as genuinely altruistic; and they are convincing, which enables them to enlist others. They are, as Oakley put it, "successfully sinister."

This personality type is rare, and its rise to political power usually occurs in a prevailing atmosphere of fear, which this personality preys upon. As we shall see in the next chapter, when Mars, or the emotional brain, is in command of the mind, fear prevails. When fear's delusional system is enforced, human beings suffer, freedom is lost, and the best in us fails to advance. Fear brings Apollo to his knees, hijacking the neural networks that engender a beautiful mind, thus diminishing reason, empathy, connection, and our sense of morality. The famous obedience experiment of Stanley Milgram at Yale University found that "ordinary people, simply doing their job, and without any particular hostility on their part, can become agents in a terrible, destructive process." They obey, "even when the destructive effects of their work are patently clear."[13] Dr. Jean Lipman-Blumen, in her book *The Allure of Toxic Leaders: Why We Follow Destructive Bosses and Corrupt Politicians—And How We Can Survive Them*, identified fear as the core of the problem. We have an underlying need for safety and belonging. People follow toxic leaders because they believe these leaders fulfill these needs and more. People refrain from challenging toxic leadership because it arouses anxiety about death and social ostracism. Toxic leaders have a genius for manipulating these needs and exploiting people's fears.

But Apollo can rise from his knees and stand. Milgram found, in a follow-up study, that the presence of a brave, fearless human being in the midst of this herd mentality can make an enormous difference. Milgram found that the presence of one person assertively refusing to follow a toxic leader into hell can bring nine out of ten anxious followers to their senses.

NOT BEING AFRAID

During the Bill Moyers PBS special *The Power of Myth*, the eminent mythologist Dr. Joseph Campbell quoted James Joyce's famous statement that "history is a nightmare from which I am trying to awake." "How do we wake up from the nightmare?" Bill Moyers asked, wide-eyed with emotion. "By not being afraid," Campbell answered, offering no further embellishment. His one-sentence answer is the complete answer. The single most powerful shift the human mind can make is the shift from fear to peace. It is people being restored to their absolute best, neurologically, psychologically, and morally. It is relationships reaching resonance. In short, it is our brain handing us the key to the good life that a healthy brain is meant to deliver. Understanding the nature of the emotional brain and how it can take over is the first step in sustaining this shift.

4

Mars, The Emotional Brain

All my life I've been like a doubled-up fist ...
Poundin', smashin', and drivin'!—now I'm going to loosen these
doubled up hands and touch things easy with them ...

Tennessee Williams

Mars, the Roman god of war, represents the emotional brain. The Romans considered Mars to be murderous and bloodstained, but also a coward. This describes one of the emotional brain's key features: fight-or-flight.

The quintessence of Mars is pure reactive power. It can take our body from deep sleep to DEFCON 1 in milliseconds. It was Mars who woke you the last time you bolted up in bed in the middle of the night from a loud sound. The pounding in your heart was Mars preparing you to fight for your life or to flee for safety. It was Apollo who eventually quieted things down with the data that the sound was just a cat knocking off the lid to the garbage can.

THE COLD, CRUEL WORLD

Every aspect of the famous bronze statue of Mars at the Gaziantep Museum captures his aggressive, defensive nature. Armed and helmeted, he stands belligerently poised against a hostile world with a snake coiled around his left arm, representing the primitive, reptilian power Mars marshals when he needs it. Mars has reason to take this posture. He is up against Planet Earth, and Earth is a dangerous place.

Mystic Cool

"It's a cold, cruel world out there," my cynical Scottish stepfather often said, "and it'll break you ... if it doesn't kill you first." In Tennessee Williams's play *Suddenly Last Summer*, the horrified Mrs. Venable vividly describes the ruthless side of the natural world.

> *Over the narrow black beach the just hatched sea turtles scrambled out of the sand pits and started their race to the sea ... to escape the flesh-eating birds that made the sky almost as black as the beach! ... And the sand all alive, all alive, as the hatched sea turtles made their dash for the sea, while the birds hovered and swooped to attack and hovered—and swooped to attack! They were diving down on the hatched sea turtles, turning them over to expose their soft undersides, tearing the undersides open and rending and eating their flesh. ... Only a hundredth of one percent of their number would escape to the sea.[1]*

The land itself, though majestic, can be just as brutal, especially to human beings. It explains the relentless effort human beings have made to push back the wilderness. Wallace Stegner, in *Wolf Willow*, describes the cold, cruel world we have struggled to tame:

> *Sometime during that roundup they may have had a day of decent weather, but it seemed to Rusty it was a procession of trials: icy nights, days when a bitter wind lashed and stung the face with a dry sand of snow, mornings when the crust flashed up a glare so blinding that they rode with eyes closed to slits and looked at the world through their eyelashes. There was one afternoon when the whole world was overwhelmed under a white freezing fog, when horses, cattle, clothes, wagon, grew a fur of hoar frost and the herd they had gathered had to be held together in spooky white darkness mainly by ear.*
>
> *On bright days they were all nearly blind, in spite of painting their cheekbones with charcoal and riding with hats pulled clear down; if they could see to work at all, they worked with tears leaking through swollen and smarting lids. Their faces grew black with sun and glare, their skin and lips cracked as crisp as the skin of a fried fish, and yet they froze.[2]*

Mother Nature can seem to be a harsh and even abusive parent, indifferent to the plight of her offspring. But this is not entirely the case. She has also stepped in to help improve the odds for survival. Millions of years ago, when life on the planet had become too complex and too dangerous for animals to navigate on instinct alone, nature evolved the brain structure called the emotional brain. The emotional brain gave the animal kingdom its initial form of intelligence. It was the highly reactive intelligence called fear.

PRIMAL FEAR

Fear, in its primal state, is quite different from the anxiety that is the source of so much trouble for human beings (we will have more to say about psychological fear later in this chapter). Primal fear is pure emotional reactivity that generates a powerful physiological response in meeting real and present danger. It is the stress response generated by the emotional brain that most of us know as fight-or-flight. It is an elaborate set of emergency neural circuits that, in a flash, heightens awareness, processes information, accelerates body activity, and produces the fuel to transform the entire system into sheer physical force. It is one of evolution's neurological wonders. Most of us have experienced the surge of primal power during an auto accident or an encounter with an aggressive dog. In a flash, body and mind come to full alert and all hands staff their battle stations. If the president of the United States assembled the world's preeminent engineers and strategists and commissioned them to develop a state-of-the-art emergency response system, they could not match even a small part of what nature put in place. In the presence of real danger, the stress response system creates Herculean strength for a brief period of time. It is the force that gives a cat a chance against a dog, and a mouse a chance against a cat. It is how a mother was once able to lift the front end of the car off of her son when he was pinned beneath it. It is the physiological surge that sustains a warrior under siege, even when wounded.

THE AMYGDALA

All of this power is under the command of Mars, and leading the charge is the part of the emotional brain called the amygdala. The amygdala is a caveman the brain has held over from our days in the wild, serving Mars as a kind of master sergeant. He is the seat of primal fear and the brain's sentry, standing guard at the perimeter for the slightest hint of approaching danger.

EMOTIONAL MEMORY

The amygdala is involved not only in the fear response but also in the memory of fear. In one test, researchers used functional MRI scans to measure amygdala activity while showing subjects a number of frightening or neutral images. They found that activity in the amygdala predicted a fear response as well as the ability to recall the frightening image several weeks later.[3] Memory is primarily what makes the emotional brain intelligent. Intelligence is, in large part, the capacity to predict, which depends on memory. The amygdala allows animals to retain information about how something threatening looked, smelled, sounded, felt, or behaved. It records what happened to help predict what works and what doesn't work in reacting to this threat. It gives animals the ability to recognize telltale signs of predators, to remember which plants are toxic, and to recall the feel of precarious terrain.

When something external activates the amygdala, it instantly scans memory for a past event that approximates this present one. If there is a rough match, the amygdala will stimulate fight-or-flight. When an event has been especially traumatic, the amygdala chemically stamps it with a stress hormone, making the memory virulent and vivid. Imagine, for example, a caveman crossing the path of a lion. As a child, he witnessed his younger sister climbing a tree to escape the beast. The emotional brain will flash in his mind the horrifying picture of the lion climbing up after his sister, dragging her to the ground, and devouring her. The warning to the caveman is obvious: don't climb a tree to escape. This emotional stamping is why we remember the details of strong emotional experiences—from something as benign as the details of a first date to something as painful as witnessing the 9/11 attack.

The model below provides a simple breakdown of how the stress response system works. When fear sounds the alarm, the adrenals pour stress hormones into the bloodstream to activate a number of systems. Heart rate, blood pressure, and respiration increase to rush extra blood and oxygen to muscles and organs. Bronchial tubes dilate to take in more oxygen, especially needed to keep the brain alert. Muscles tighten, initially freezing the body. Energy stores breakdown fat, glucose, and protein to dump them into the bloodstream to fuel the large muscles.

The brain, now rich with oxygenated blood, sharpens our senses. We hear acutely. Our eyes dilate to take in more light and a wider visual field. Remember how hyper-alert you became the last time you saw a horror movie? We can even experience altered states of awareness, as in an auto accident, when details appear in slow motion frames, even through it all happens in a flash.

Simple Model of a Stress Response

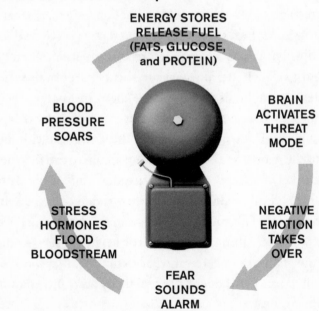

THREAT MODE

When the amygdala senses the world creeping up on us, it locks the brain in threat mode. It is what makes some animals jittery, constantly scanning the environment, reacting to the smallest change. In human infants, the amygdala is well developed at birth, far more than the neocortex. This is why infants are so easily startled. Evolution's aim was to provide infants with a direct way of communicating their basic needs for survival. When an infant is frightened, hungry, uncomfortable, or sick, the amygdala sets off an emotional reaction to get a parent's attention. When the amygdala is in the throes of a stress response, it activates an attentional bias for threat. This means eyes and ears will scan the immediate environment for other potential dangers. A zebra or wildebeest, being chased from behind by a lion, remembers that lions hunt in prides. Thus, its brain will scan the field for lions approaching from other directions.

LIGHTNING SPEED

The amygdala is also lightning fast, with a reaction time that is, perhaps, twice that of the neocortex. Once fully activated, the amygdala does not readily retreat when Apollo advises that, in this situation, discretion is the better part of valor. To the amygdala, the better part of valor is a club or a speedy retreat. He holds first position, ahead of Apollo, whenever there is any question of security. The research of Joseph LeDoux discovered brain pathways taking information into the amygdala without first going through the neocortex. Nature wired the brain to fire first and ask questions later. LeDoux points out that freezing is often the first fear response people and other animals have when sudden danger appears. "Predators respond to movement," LeDoux stated, "so freezing is overall probably the best single thing to do first, at least it was for our distant ancestors. If they had to think about what to do first, they would have been so caught up in the thought process that they'd probably fidget around and then get eaten."[4]

A scientist tried to see if he could get the neocortex, which is in charge of voluntary functions, to override the amygdala. He put a rattlesnake in a thick glass cage where it could not harm anyone. He had one hundred subjects put their faces close to the glass, and the scientist then provoked the snake to make it strike. Every time the snake struck the glass, the subjects jerked back: one hundred out of one hundred. They could not control or alter their reaction. A primal stress reaction was designed to be involuntary in order to save our hides.

Assuming the Worst

Another of Mars's mythological offspring is Dread. This characteristic describes the tendency of Mars, or the emotional brain, to assume the worst whenever things feel unsafe. Assuming the worst in the wild or in war is, from evolution's standpoint, the best bet, given how unforgiving indecision is in the face of danger.

Negative Emotion

Mars also sanctioned the amygdala to inflame negative emotion. He has a license to hate. From evolution's point of view, hate and savagery trump loving kindness when a predator with sharp teeth is about to tear into our body. The American novelist Willa Cather in her masterpiece *My Ántonia* describes the intense emotion the amygdala can generate in her depiction of an encounter with a rattlesnake:

> *He was as thick as my leg, and looked as if millstones couldn't crush the disgusting vitality out of him. He lifted his hideous little head, and rattled. I didn't run because I didn't think of it—if my back had been against a stone wall I couldn't have felt more cornered. I saw his coils tighten—now it would spring, spring with length, I remembered. I ran up and drove at his head with my spade, struck him fairly across the*

neck, and in a minute he was all about my feet in wavy loops. I struck now from hate.... Even after I had pounded his ugly head flat, his body kept coiling and winding, doubling and falling back on itself. I walked away and turned my back. I felt seasick.[5]

THE FIVE-MINUTE WINDOW

The seasick feeling is the result of the toll a full-blown stress reaction has on the body. For about five minutes it makes all living creatures stronger, faster, meaner, and more alert, in order to meet a threat. But the body can only handle the biochemical flood and its physiological impact for five minutes before systems start to break down. It is hard on the body, and stress hormones are toxic to the brain. The stress response system also shuts down the digestive, immune, reproductive, and other long-term systems to commandeer their energy for the short term. A million years ago, when Homo sapiens first emerged in the wild, the five-minute clock on a stress response told the tale. In that time, we would either prevail, escape, or be killed.

MARS AND MODERN MAN

But what is the nature of a stress response for modern people? It is rarely wild animals. Rather, it is emotional threats to our sense of safety. The wild animals that overwhelm us now are anxiety about our livelihood, fear of failure, constant change, perceived insults to our sense of dignity, conflicts with people, disobedient children, multitasking, swelling to-do lists, traffic jams, and computer malfunctions, to name a few.

STRESS

Neuroscience labels these modern afflictions "stress" precisely because they set off a stress reaction. All of these problems carry some form of fear and, as we have seen, fear and the reactive amygdala go hand in hand. Stress and fear are biologically linked. When stress is chronic, as it is with 40 percent of Americans, it is an indication that Mars has staged a coup on Apollo.

PSYCHOLOGICAL FEAR

BODY IN AN UPROAR

PERCEIVED THREAT

NEGATIVE EMOTION

FEARFUL THINKING

By far, the fear driving stress reactions in the civilized world is psychological, not primal. Psychological fear is the edgy interplay of fearful thinking and emotion that haunts the mind with the misperception of threat and risk. It essentially mistakes a stick for a snake, triggering the same fight-or-flight response as primal fear.

Robert Sapolsky of Stanford University stated in *Why Zebras Don't Get Ulcers*: "We humans ... are smart enough to generate all sorts of stressful events purely in our heads.... We can experience wildly strong emotions (provoking our bodies into an accompanying uproar) linked to mere thoughts."[6]

In my community, there is a homeless man who behaves in ways that most people would label mentally disturbed. In the mornings, he walks the street in front of the local coffee house where we, the mentally sound, stop to get a double dose of gourmet caffeine before heading to work. A long line for coffee forms and extends out onto the sidewalk, where this homeless man does his pacing. Up and down the block he walks, usually with a wild look in his eyes, talking incessantly to himself about something that never seems to make any sense. Often his tone is angry, and every now and then he stops and shakes his head in frustration at something he has imagined. Those of us who have become used to this man smile and look at each other with amusement. Those catching his act for the first time anxiously step back to avoid contact.

Few of us see ourselves in this spectacle. Few of us acknowledge that we have similar disturbances going on in our heads all the time. We just hide our delusional system better than he hides his. If neuroscience invented an audio system that was hooked up to our thoughts and could broadcast them for the world to hear, not one of us would volunteer to wear it to church, or to a cocktail party, or down to the corner market.

After an encounter with this homeless man, some of us get into cars, drink the strong coffee that kicks incessant thinking into high speed, and enter the private world of our own anxiety. We may even have a full-blown conversation with an adversary, all of it carried on in our heads. We might script an entire drama, putting words in the other person's mouth and then constructing clever comebacks that lay her to waste. At times, this imaginary process may even excite a strong stress reaction, depleting our energy. When we get to work and see the person with whom we have had the imaginary conversation, we might throw them a cold shoulder, as if the experience we made up in the car had actually happened. The fact is, to the amygdala it did happen. The amygdala cannot tell the difference between primal fear and psychological fear. It sets off a stress reaction when either is present. For modern people, stress reactions are largely triggered by psychologically induced fears to mind-made emergencies, many of which are illusions.

> **I've been through some terrible things in my life,**
> **some of which actually happened.**
> Mark Twain

When we are chronically stressed, everything outlined in this chapter becomes our experience, from emotional memories projecting the past onto the present and forecasting a future that is worse, to emotional negativity exciting the bias for threat, to strong physical reactions that tax the body and drain our energy.

Don Joseph Goewey

EMOTIONAL MEMORY: TRAPPED IN THE PAST

As already mentioned, the amygdala learns to recognize and remember danger. When the fear exciting the memory is psychological fear, the odds of misperceiving the situation increase. When we are chronically stressed, meaning when psychological fear is persistent, we can become trapped in the past. In conditioning experiments conducted by Joseph LeDoux, rats were repeatedly given a mild electric shock in conjunction with an auditory tone.[7] Eventually, the rats associated the sound with the pain, reacting fearfully when the tone alone was sounded. They showed all the signs of fight-or-flight: freezing in place, high blood pressure, and rapid breathing. The rats essentially were afraid of the past. It is the same in human beings. When we are anxious and stressed, an innocuous sound, sight, or person that the amygdala associates with a past trauma can trigger a negative reaction. The amygdala is making quick and dirty guesses, like in a game of charades. It is often the wrong guess, causing behavior that can be regrettably inappropriate.

Years ago, an agency I directed had conducted an exhaustive hiring process for a high-level position. A team of people had selected two candidates for me to interview, a man and a woman, and they strongly recommended that I hire the man. After interviewing both, I hired the woman. I didn't like the man. In fact, I disliked him intensely. He looked and even behaved like the fellow who, in my youth, had stolen my sweetheart away. My amygdala kicked up the emotional pain of that past event, and I just couldn't get above it. Even though he was superior to the other candidate, I sent him away. I didn't want him around to remind me of a pain that in reality had nothing to do with him. A similar reaction happened when my daughter dated a boy who resembled another nemesis from my past. Often these associations are subliminal.

However, the research of Joe Zsien at Princeton has shown that rats can learn to be unafraid of what they had once been conditioned to fear, like LeDoux's rats, and rather quickly.[8] The sound becomes just a sound again. So can human beings. We can break these associations by conditioning ourselves to remember that the fear is in us, not reality.

THE ATTENTIONAL BIAS FOR THREAT

When we are stressed, the amygdala kicks into an attentional bias for threat. Like the zebra being chased, when we feel threatened we scan the immediate environment for who might attack us from the side. This can also cause us to misperceive people and events in unfortunate ways. A colleague, for example, recently faced a difficult meeting with her board of directors, in which she was scheduled to present a progress report. The outcomes were not as promising as she had hoped. She was especially concerned about one member of the board whom she described as mean-spirited. During her presentation, her adversary made a critical remark in what my friend perceived as an insulting tone of voice. My friend's fear level immediately escalated, exciting the amygdala to full alert. Stress hormones flooded her bloodstream, and her heart rate accelerated. To the amygdala, her adversary was akin to a wild animal. A few moments later, the adversary leaned over and whispered into the ear of the person next to him, who shook her head and frowned in disgust. My friend's amygdala went into attentional bias for threat, widening its wary eye to keep track of this second person. It was two days before my friend took this second person off her terrorist list, when she learned that what had been shared was simply the closing figure for the Dow Jones that day.

THE ABSENCE OF A METABOLIC MATCH

Additionally, when we were in the wild and experienced a full-blown stress reaction, usually we were clawing, kicking, swinging, or running for our life. There was a metabolic match to the event, burning all the fuels, stress hormones, and other junk dumped into the bloodstream. But stress reactions for modern people usually happen at our desk when our computer glitches, at a conference table during a difficult meeting, in our car in the middle of a traffic jam, or at home in a toe-to-toe argument with our spouse. There is no physical exertion burning the stuff that a stress reaction releases, and the pool of stress hormones can take hours to reabsorb. During that time the brain remains neurotoxic.

For a zebra, when danger passes, it goes back to munching the grass. The zebra doesn't bend the ear of any zebra willing to listen, kvetching with: "Why did God make lions? Why does the world have to be so unsafe? Can't you see we are all going to die?" The zebra's nervous system automatically switches from sympathetic (stress mode) to parasympathetic (homeostasis), and it calmly returns to normal without giving the event another thought. Stress hormones have cleared his system, burned off from all the running. All the important systems, like immunity and digestion, which were dampened to commandeer energy for flight-or-fight, now return to normal. We human beings, on the other hand, tend to ruminate after a stressful event, prolonging a stress reaction. It taxes the body, debilitates the brain, and eventually makes us ill.

DISSECTING PSYCHOLOGICAL FEAR

There are four basic forms of psychological fear that are worth reviewing.

General Anxiety

General anxiety is experienced as a fretful, nameless, and often formless uneasiness. It is the fear for one's safety, well-being, and livelihood, representing an underlying belief that the world is no longer a safe place. Anxiety spawns many feelings—awkwardness, agitation, restlessness, worry, complete overwhelm—all validating the belief that who we are and what we have is not good enough. We tend to mistake anxiety as a reaction to something out there instead of a fearful disposition inside that is distorting reality. Compounding matters is how much value our society places on fear. Governments, management, the movie industry, the news media, and even religions drill fear into us. Albert Camus, 1957 Nobel laureate in literature, said, "Our twentieth century is the century of fear."[9] As we move deeper into the twenty-first century, it is clear that fear is not in decline.

The Hairpin Trigger

The hairpin trigger is the most visible and perhaps the most destructive manifestation of psychological fear. It occurs when a flash from the past, a snap judgment, a misperception, or a buildup of negative sentiment arouses a bolt of emotion. The amygdala, ever on guard, ordains our distorted perception as fact, and fires. Emotions suddenly erupt in an aggressive or defensive flare that hijacks all rational thought. Before we know it, we have reacted in a way that we will later regret and that can even ruin our life. Crimes of passion occur in this way. Almost half of all murders are committed when an acquaintance or relative of the victim goes insane with rage.[10] More than a quarter of all women murdered are killed by boyfriends or husbands. Drugs and alcohol can also make us volatile; 60 percent of murders happen when people are intoxicated.[11]

Generally when stress is high, anger is the first emotion that is triggered—either with oneself, toward others, or with a situation.[12] Most of the time, however, no one gets physically assaulted by this form of unleashed fear.

Eruptions, when they do occur, can last for a moment, or they can go on for an unbearable period of time, as in rage. The emotion can be retriggered or even amplified by the reactions of others, even when they are attempting to calm things down. When the full power of the amygdala is set loose, it is not easily contained. The shock wave from these destructive emotions rattles the body to its core, weakening and even damaging it. The effect on the entire system can last for days and, of course, relationships can be ruptured for life.

The hairpin trigger can also occur without overt volatility, as in a terse word spoken under breath, a telling look, or an abrupt departure. Nevertheless, there is a charged energy to the act that is unmistakable to the person on the receiving end.

Moodiness

Some days we wake up in a bad mood, often without a clue as to why. When we get up to make coffee, the bad mood follows us into the kitchen. It mumbles away as we take our shower. It makes us angry when we can't find the shoes that match the clothes we've selected for the day. On the ride to work it chastises the world for every inconvenience and scowls at anyone who dares to be happy. Loved ones irritate us, colleagues seem incompetent, children are annoying, the elderly are fumblers, and life in general seems to conspire against us. A bad mood clouds us like the dust that surrounds Pigpen from the "Peanuts" comic strip. There is nothing much we are going to like that day. It drives the better angels of our nature into hiding, and it can be difficult to get them to return. We usually have to wait for them to come back on their own, when the atmosphere is conducive to the peace and optimism of a good mood.

One can be sure that Mars, the emotional brain, is behind the bad mood. Mars is afraid of the world; there is much about the world that he does not like or trust. Every now and then, for no apparent reason, Mars goes dark. He elbows Apollo out of the way in disgust, stomps on all of Apollo's good work, blames the world and everyone in it for the mood, and rains on as many parades as he can find.

Self-Righteousness

Psychological fear can also make us unreasonable and arrogant. Mars does not question his perceptions. As we have seen, Mars and his henchman, the amygdala, do not wait patiently for the cogent facts to fall into place. Unlike the reasonable and thoughtful Apollo, Mars does not try to understand, consider another's point of view, feel empathy, give the benefit of the doubt, include, or negotiate. The nature of his power is not assertive like Apollo's. His power is aggressive. The central aim of Mars is the elimination of threat. When Mars is in charge of our mind, he can make us overly controlling or even pompous. He can cause us to take a fixed, unyielding position, or continue to argue a point needlessly. We believe we are right and others are wrong; we are more and they are less. At times, being right can go as far as wanting those who disagree with us to be removed altogether. Make no mistake; the militant nature of the amygdala perceives losing an argument as losing the war, not figuratively but literally. We think we are arguing over a point, but an excited amygdala believes we are fighting for our life.

> When I say manage emotions, I only mean the really distressing, incapacitating emotions.
> Daniel Goleman

THE PRICE WE PAY

The price we pay for turning our lives over to Mars and his penchant for setting off stress reactions is manifold. Chronic stress can make the brain neurotoxic with stress hormones. Stress hormones can dampen, and even knock out, a number of brain functions that enable us to perform well.[13] Studies on human performance have found that the greater the stress, the greater the likelihood we will choose risky alternatives or make premature decisions. Immediate survival goals will replace long-range considerations. There will be a tendency toward aggression and escape behaviors. We will be less tolerant of ambiguity, communication channels will close, and creative thinking will fail to reach an end result because we are more likely to give up too soon.[14] Transcend stress, and all these functions, which represent neural circuits, come back on line.

Perhaps the greatest impact of chronic stress on the brain occurs in the hippocampus. The hippocampus keeps our daily lives on track. It is responsible for the formation of declarative, episodic, and spatial memory. Declarative memory stores the dry facts. It is as dry as textbook learning or a grocery list. Episodic memory has a little more drama to it. It helps us keep track of people and events in our daily life—what happened to us, people we encountered, and information we gathered. Spatial memory is the brain's GPS. It holds all the various road maps we have in our head that get us from here to there without much thought. The brains of metropolitan taxi cab drivers develop a larger hippocampus to store all the spatial memories they need to get their passengers to the correct location. Spatial memory also keeps track of places where we've squirreled away important items, like a passport or a diamond necklace.

The hippocampus appears to be the first system to falter when stress hormones get too high. When we have a spell where increasingly we can't remember where we put our keys, why we opened the kitchen cabinet, or momentarily lose track of where we are, it is probably because our level of stress is impairing the hippocampus. The hippocampus also appears to work hand in hand with the amygdala to keep things in context, adding the correct emotional climate to the dry facts to keep us from being inappropriate. It reminds a man's testosterone that the attractive woman sitting across from him at the meeting is the boss. Transcend stress, and the brain helps us behave appropriately.

Chronic stress also retards neurogenesis, which is the capacity of the hippocampus to make new brain cells. The hippocampus generates new brain cells, in part, to capture novel experiences. Novel experiences, when remembered, enable us see life in a fresh new way. Without the means to retain new experiences, life can become monotonous, dull, and ultimately depressing. It is now thought that the inability to capture novel experiences through neurogenesis may actually be a factor in depression. Theoretically, if we transcend stress, we will make new brain cells. Transcending stress, in itself, will generate all sorts of novel experiences. In this stress-free environment, the hippocampus will store these new experiences in new brain cells, and these memories will then act as an antidote to our depression. Life will make sense again.

Chronic stress impairs the production of serotonin, a neurotransmitter that plays an important role in stabilizing mood and modulating the impulse to anger and aggression.[15] It is also involved in body temperature, sleep, sexuality, appetite, and metabolism. Changes in serotonin levels in the brain are associated with depression and the tendency to multiply common everyday problems into hopeless calamities that drain the spirit dry. Life becomes gray and lackluster, work loses its meaning, and relationships fail to produce closeness.

Depletion of serotonin also appears to decrease our capacity for win-win. We just don't see the reward in trusting others, playing fair, and cooperating.[16] In a study at Oxford, researchers engaged subjects in a two-person game known as the Prisoner's Dilemma. As the game unfolds, players eventually have to choose between a move that wins one player money at the expense of their partner, or make a move that maximizes money for both. In the end, the best strategy for making money in this game is cooperation. Under normal circumstances, people realize this and go for win-win 75 percent of the time. In the study, however, half the subjects were given a drink that depleted tryptophan, an amino acid that synthesizes serotonin, thereby decreasing serotonin levels in their brain. The researchers found that dampening serotonin activity significantly decreased the level of cooperation and trust among the players. "The findings suggest that a serotonin deficit might impair sustained cooperation," said Dr. Robert Rogers, the chief investigator of the study.[17] This negatively impacts not only teamwork at the office but married couples trying to build a life together. Transcend stress, and serotonin will naturally make us want to be a better person.

Dopamine is another neurotransmitter that chronic social stress impacts.[18] Whereas serotonin is the humble and happy sage of neurotransmitters, promoting grace and equanimity, dopamine is Zorba the Greek, high on life, joyful, self-confident, and motivated. The higher people's levels of dopamine, the more positive their feelings.[19] Dopamine is commonly associated with the pleasure system of the brain, providing feelings of enjoyment and reinforcement to motivate us to be proactive in our lives. It is also involved in sleep, attention, and learning. When levels are out of balance because of chronic stress, we lose our zest for life. Transcend stress, and our brain starts to reestablish the chemistry to care about life again.

Perhaps the most noticeable effect of repeated stress reactions is low energy; chronic stress leaves us listless and fatigued. Fatigue is the number one symptom that Americans assign to stress.[20] By midday we can feel physically and emotionally spent. A buildup of stress hormones combined with falling serotonin levels can keep us from achieving deeper levels of restful sleep, trapping us in a vicious cycle of fatigue. Transcend stress, and the bounce returns to our step.

Another telltale feature of chronic stress is emotional negativity. Biologically, the stress response kicks the brain into negative emotions and locks the brain into threat mode. When that happens, we are likely to blame and defend and even become aggressive. One in four people in a national survey of nearly two thousand respondents reported that during the last five years their personal relationships have suffered because of stress. Alienation from friends topped the list.[21] Forty-two percent of us also report that work stress is negatively affecting the quality of family life,[22] which, in turn, is affecting the normal adjustment of children and adolescents.[23]

Ellen Galinsky of the Family and Work Institute studied a nationally representative sample of more than six hundred parents and one thousand children, ranging from third to twelfth grade. Jeanna Bryner of the Associated Press reported:

> *Interviewers asked children what would be their one wish if they could change how a father or mother's work affected each child. More than half of parents guessed their children would wish for more parent time. Wrong answer. Most children wished their parents would be less stressed from work. "If our parents were less tired and stressed, I think that the kids would be less tired and stressed," said one of the children interviewed.... Subtle cues, such as a parent's down-turned expression or heavy footsteps, also led kids to easily detect their parents' moods. "I know when my mom has a bad day because when she picks me up from after school she doesn't smile," one young girl told interviewers. "She has a really frustrated look on her face."[24]*

Transcend stress and we smile more and love more.

As most of know firsthand, stress also makes us sick. There are one million people out of work every day due to stress disorders.[25] As already mentioned, stress reactions dampen long-range systems, temporarily borrowing their energy supply to fuel fight-or-flight. When stress reactions are chronic, the deficit mounts, causing trouble. A persistent dampening of the immune system leads to a greater susceptibility to colds and flu. Infection occurs more frequently, tends to be more severe, and can recur more readily. A buildup of stress hormones in the bloodstream can result in rashes. A weakened reproductive system can lead to sexual apathy and dysfunction. A compromised digestive system can result in gastrointestinal problems and, of course, stress leads to tightening of muscles, causing the perennial tension headache, stiff neck, and sore back. Chronic stress is also associated with hair loss.

Stress reactions shut down the growth system, inhibiting the production of growth hormones that generate new hair. Our hair thins out and spots develop. The lost hair may eventually grow back but often it comes back gray. When I was a child, my mother sometimes complained that her five rambunctious children were turning her hair gray. It turns out she was right.

When stress reactions happen week in, week out, month after month for years, it can lead to premature aging. Stress reactions can wear down the heart and damage the cardiovascular system. Everything we define as well-being depends on our emotional response to specific events. One of the most compelling demonstrations of this association was a study of nearly thirty thousand patients from fifty-two countries, assessing the impact of nine conventional risk factors for heart attack such as hypertension, abdominal obesity, diabetes, and several other traditional risk factors.[26] Chronic stress conferred a greater adjusted relative risk of acute myocardial infarction than any other factor. A high level of stress increases the relative risk of a heart attack by two-and-a-half fold, compared with a low level of stress. The list of stress-related illnesses is not limited to heart disease. All the short-term, acute health problems cited above can become chronic in nature as each of the dampened systems gradually weakens. The list of illnesses that can develop is long. It includes immunodeficiency, type 2 diabetes, reproductive disorders, obesity, osteoporosis, and ulcers. One hundred years ago the major causes of death among Americans were bacteria, viruses, and childbirth. Today a stress-related disease is likely to do us in. Transcend stress and we will live longer.

Stress is also making Jenny Craig rich. Stress causes the body to put on weight more readily. During a stress reaction, adrenaline forces the release of fuel from energy stores into the bloodstream to energize fight-or-flight. When the stress reaction subsides, another stress hormone, cortisol, sees to it that the stores are replenished. Unfortunately, cortisol makes its deposits in the fat bin. When this hormone is persistently high, fat starts to accumulate around the abdomen and in the walls of blood vessels that have been cracked and pitted by the force of repeated stress reactions. Compounding the problem is the tendency of people to reach for high fat and high carbohydrate comfort food during bouts of stress. Transcend stress and we might lose a few pounds without breaking a sweat.

How Big Is the Problem?

It is bad news all the way down. The problem of stress is pervasive. If the Centers for Disease Control and Prevention classified stress as a disease, they would have to declare it an epidemic. Gallup's annual Lifestyle poll found that four out of ten people experience high levels of stress frequently.[27] Another four struggle with stress, but less frequently. To put this in the context of an average company, it means that, periodically, eight on a team of ten people managing an important project are likely to be emotionally negative, aggressive, or withdrawn, choosing risky alternatives, and struggling with memory loss, attention deficit, and poor error detection. One of the team is likely to be home, sick. In the next six months, one will quit, with a one-in-two chance that the reason is stress. Half will take their stress home and suffer family discord, returning to work the next day more rattled than the day before. This is hardly the picture of a high-performance project team. It is a far cry from Aristotle's good life. No wonder only 47 percent of Americans are satisfied with their jobs, a sizable drop from the 61 percent who expressed satisfaction twenty years ago.[28]

Spouses and Parents

Nearly half of parents say they frequently experience stress in their daily lives and, as discussed, it is affecting the quality of their parenting.[29] People also report that stress is taking a toll on their marriages, leading to discord.

Young Adults

A study in England has also found that stress-related illness is now affecting people earlier in life. The study followed a group of one thousand children born in 1972–73 throughout their lives. At age thirty-two, the subjects were asked about their work. Those with "high psychological demands" at work were 75 percent more likely to suffer from depression or anxiety. In addition, at age thirty-two, one in eight was diagnosed with clinical depression, anxiety disorders, or both for the first time in their lives.[30]

Leaders

Nearly 90 percent of people in corporate leadership positions report that work is the primary source of stress in their lives. Two-thirds state they are more stressed than five years ago. Yet, 60 percent say their organizations fail to provide the tools they need to effectively manage stress. Ironically, the greater part of the stress these leaders experience is not from external factors, such as a lack of resources or an unmanageable to-do list. Eighty-three percent cite manifestations of psychological fear as the primary cause of their stress. This includes conflict, issues of trust, politics, confrontations, relationship problems, personal insecurity, style differences, and an imbalance of work and family.[31]

Doctors and Nurses

Almost half of all nurses, doctors, and lab technicians report that most days at work are quite or extremely stressful. Nursing supervisors are among those reporting the highest on-the-job stress. Two-thirds of head nurses and nurse supervisors report high work stress.[32] The biggest source of stress for doctors, according to a study of more than three thousand physicians, is the anxiety of having made a mistake along with the fear of committing more errors.[33]

Students and Teachers

One recent study found that one out of three teachers surveyed described their jobs as extremely stressful, and that stressed teachers can hinder a child's education.[34] Since 1997, there has also been a sharp increase in the level of stress among college students nationwide. A thirteen-year study of more than thirteen thousand students at Kansas

State University found that, between the academic years of 1988 to 2000, the number of students with depression and suicidal thoughts doubled, along with the number of students dealing with stress-related health problems.[35]

It's All of Us

Stress is serious and it plagues all of us. It makes us sick, dampens our intelligence, and drains the joy out of life. It takes us in the opposite direction of the good life. Stress has become such an ingrained part of our vocabulary and daily existence that it is hard to believe that use of the term originated little more than fifty years ago, with the publication in 1956 of *The Stress of Life* by Hans Selye, the father of stress research. Back then, it was a term used by engineers, not physicians. When Selye was asked to present a paper in France, he found that there was no word in French for stress, so he coined *le stress*. He found the same to be true in Germany, and named it *der Stress*.

Stress has always been with us; we have just referred to it by other names. The condition of chronic stress is to modern life what the concept of suffering is to Buddhism; or the fall from grace is to Muslims, Jews, and Christians. It represents a dominance of fear that drains life of peace, joy, and well-being. Neurologically, chronic stress represents a brain dominated by the amygdala, wired for survival.

IS IT HOPELESS?

No, it is not hopeless; far from it. We can escape these problems. As we shall see in the next chapter, we can actually rewire our brains to override Mars and empower Apollo. A change of mind can literally change the brain. It is called neuroplasticity, and the change can happen faster than you might think—with practice, in a matter of weeks. We can learn to transcend stress and, in so doing, build the brain structure for an optimal experience of life and work. We can learn to use the power of Mars to enrich life instead of allowing the reactive side of Mars to hijack our happiness. Apollo can dip into Mars's well of emotion, evolving wonderful feelings like passion, inspiration, and all the forms of love out of the swamp of primal fear. This partnership is what inspires or excites us to act. It is the feeling of anticipation that sits at the edge of a new vision. It is the enthusiasm in a goal. It is the deep affection in a committed relationship and the unconditional devotion of a mother to her child. It signals what feels right, as well as whom and what we can trust. When Apollo and Mars harmonize, we start to feel our way to answers that too much intellect complicates and too much emotion clouds.

5

The Mystical Brain

The most beautiful emotion we can experience is the mysterious.
It is the fundamental emotion that stands at the cradle of all true
art and science. He to whom this emotion is a stranger, who can
no longer wonder and stand rapt in awe, is as good as dead,
a snuffed-out candle.

Albert Einstein

In 1987, His Holiness the Dalai Lama, recipient of the Nobel Peace Prize and spiritual leader of Tibetan Buddhism, joined forces with leading researchers to establish the Mind and Life Institute.[1] The aim of the institute is to foster dialogue and research between modern science and the great living contemplative traditions. Over the course of these meetings, the Dalai Lama periodically posed this question to neuroscientists: could the mind change the brain? It is a critical question. If the answer is no, it means the brain is the ultimate mechanism that establishes our experience in life. It means the brain directs our lives according to the way it is wired, imposing a limit on the potential for happiness, growth, and success. If you believe that the brain creates the mind and that brain structure is fixed, then the answer you would give the Dalai Lama is no, nothing changes the brain once its structure is set. That was what the scientists believed at the time and that was the answer they gave.

The version of the immutable brain that relates to the individual we become is called the mood set point. This theory states that our baseline or signature attitude through which we view, approach, and experience life is also fixed in rigid brain structure. Thus, significant, sustainable change in personality or basic attitude is not possible, so the theory goes. If nature, social conditioning, and poor quality of nurturing during childhood wire a person's brain for fear, then fight-or-flight and the stress it causes are likely to dominate a person's life. The way she is wired will ultimately sabotage the choice to free her life from a painful past, change direction, or transform her attitude. Self-defeating becomes brain-defeated. Anxious, critical, and unhappy parents, who inadvertently wire us for a pessimistic disposition, doom us to die whining. If faulty brain wiring creates obsessive, compulsive, or depressed tendencies in a person, there can be no cure. It is a hopeless picture for the distressed, which, as the data in the last chapter indicates, is most of us.

The belief that the brain does not change led to a growing disregard within neuroscience for psychology and spirituality. After all, if you believe that the brain creates the mind, that it is also fixed and in a state of gradual decline, then it follows that there is no neurological basis for psychology and spirituality, which aims for personality change, self-improvement, and growth. Even the respected cognitive neuroscientist and popular author Michael S. Gazzaniga stated as recently as 1998 that "psychology itself is dead."[2]

For the last hundred years, the immutable brain was science's view. Science believed from the evidence it gathered that brain structure was the hand we were dealt and, like it or not, the hand we would play for life. Worse, given the old belief that brains do not generate new cells, it follows that gradually we would lose intelligence as cells die. The doctrine of the immutable brain was established in the nineteenth century by Nobel laureate Santiago Ramon y Cajal. During the twentieth century Ramon y Cajal's doctrine was canon. Here is what he said:

> Once the development was ended, the founts of growth and regeneration of the axons and dendrites dried up irrevocably. In the adult centers, the nerve paths are something fixed, ended, and immutable. Everything may die, nothing may be regenerated. It is for the science of the future to change, if possible, this harsh decree.[3]

There was another point of view at that time, articulated by the seminal French psychologist Alfred Binet, inventor of the first intelligence quotient (IQ) test. Binet wrote:

A few modern philosophers and scientists assert that an individual's intelligence is a fixed property, a quantity which cannot be increased. I protest and react against this brutal pessimism.... With practice, training, and above all, method, we manage to increase our attention, our memory, our judgment and literally become more intelligent then we were before.[4]

Binet's assertion didn't get any further with the scientists of his time than the Dalai Lama got with modern scientist. Modern science stubbornly held to the old dogma. The mind cannot change the brain, most of them told the Dalai Lama. Nothing can, they said.

The good news is neuroscience has had a complete change of mind. It now asserts that scientists like Binet were correct and those like Ramon y Cajal were incorrect. By the 1980s, "neuroscientists had accumulated a compelling body of evidence that the brain is dynamic: remodeling itself continually in response to experience."[5] Charles Sherrington in 1912, Ivory Franz in 1915, Karl Lasky in 1923, Donald Hebb in 1949, Michael Merzenich in 1985, and other researchers have clearly demonstrated that you can teach an old monkey new tricks and that the brain would restructure, rewire, rebuild, and rezone areas of the cortex to strengthen new competencies. By 1996, Elizabeth Gould at Princeton had also toppled the entrenched canon of neuroscience when she proved that the primate brain creates new neurons continuously.[6] This was followed in 1998 by the discovery of Peter Eriksson of Göteborg University, who found that "the human hippocampus retains its ability to generate neurons throughout life."[7] It is called neurogenesis, which means the brain can generate the raw material for changing or strengthening the system.

MENTAL PRACTICE

By the mid-1990s, research had already demonstrated that the brain responds to the mind when given direction. When so directed, the brain can take a small village of neurons and turn it into a humming metropolis. The term given to this wonderful neurological property is *neuroplasticity*. It is the mechanism that provides a monkey with the dexterity to retrieve a banana pellet from a tight spot. Neuroplasticity even works with imagination to learn, build, and strengthen difficult skillsets, such as playing the piano. In 1995, a neuroscientist at Harvard named Alvaro Pascual-Leone demonstrated this. He instructed subjects to play a five-finger piano exercise two hours every day for five days. At the end of each practice session, Pascual-Leone measured the motor cortex of the brain that controls precise finger movement. The data revealed that at the end of the five days, the amount of motor cortex devoted to the finger movements had spread, taking over surrounding areas of the brain. At the same time, Pascual-Leone had another group simply think about practicing the five-finger piano exercise. They played the simple piece over and over in their minds, keeping their fingers still and simply imagining how their fingers would move if actually playing the piano. The results were astonishing. The area of motor cortex had expanded in the imaginary players in the same way it had in subjects who had actually played the piano. "Mental practice," Pascual-Leone stated, "resulted in a similar reorganization" of the brain.[8]

Neuroplasticity also has been shown to restore peace of mind in people afflicted with mental illness. Research has established that a fundamental shift in attitude actually directs the brain to alter circuits in ways that transform the daily experience of people suffering from obsessive-compulsive disorder (OCD) and chronic depression. In 1987, Dr. Jeffrey Schwartz of UCLA used nothing more than a change of mind to change the faulty brain wiring that causes OCD. OCD is marked by hyperactivity in the orbitofrontal cortex, which is the part of the brain associated with punishment and detecting errors. When it is hyperactive, it causes a person to become overwhelmed by the sense that something is wrong. This, in turn, triggers hyperactivity in another part of brain, called the striatum. In OCD, the striatum receives both the error message from the orbital frontal cortex and a jolt of dread from an aroused amygdala. This makes the situation feel dreadfully wrong and excites a gripping need to act.

These three neural systems string together to form what is called the worry circuit. It is incredibly debilitating. People wash their hands incessantly, walk ritualistically in between the squares on the sidewalk, or turn the car around and head back home to make sure the stove is off, even when memory assures that the stove is not on. OCD patients often feel as if these thoughts and compulsions do not come from their real self; it feels as if an alien force has taken possession of their mind.

In his landmark study, Schwartz had patients use their mind to heal their brains. None were taking medication during the trials. Instead, Schwartz simply showed patients PET scans of the hyperactive parts of their brain to prove to them that OCD was faulty neurological wiring. He then formed a therapy group to help patients practice relabeling their obsessive thoughts and weird compulsions as a malfunction of the brain. As calmly as possible, they observed their dire thoughts and sensations, and then refuted each by stating: "This is not me. It is my brain generating another obsessive thought. I know it is not real; it is just the garbage thrown up by a faulty circuit." Remarkably, one week into the process of relabeling their symptoms as brain glitches, patients reported the disease no longer controlled them. They felt that now there was something they could do to effectively intervene. Schwartz then performed new PET scans to ascertain if this remarkable shift was accompanied by changes in brain activity. PET scans from twelve of the eighteen members of the group showed activity in the orbital frontal cortex had fallen significantly compared to the scans at the outset of the study.[9]

A similar approach was found to work with depression.[10] A major problem with depression is relapse following treatment. It does not take much to trigger a relapse. A small setback can ignite a rash of pessimistic thinking and self-condemnation, as one thought cascades over another until a person is lost in a hopeless, helpless collapse of self-confidence. Something as minor as a terse word from a boss can devolve into thinking, *I am worthless*, followed by, *my life is a failure*. This kind of negative thinking can proliferate, draining the life out of a person. Everything he sees, thinks, or feels bears witness to a bleak reality. It is a mind-made reality, and it seems the brain follows the mind straight into hell by wiring for stress, fear, and negativity.

In 1992, Zindel Segal at the University of Toronto began to investigate ways of preventing relapse, using cognitive behavioral therapy (CBT). CBT is a highly directed, short-term set of lessons that raise the awareness of negative, fearful thinking in order to refute it sensibly, with realistic facts. With depression, emotion becomes reality, and stressful, fearful thoughts become facts. Segal taught his patients to relate to their depression simply as events of the mind. They learned strategies for breaking the tendency to ruminate over a problem, to interpret small setbacks as major calamities, or to turn possible outcomes into catastrophes. They practiced taking greater responsibility for their moods, acknowledging that often people and events are not causing their upsets, but rather their own thoughts, feelings, and attitudes about people and events are. The subjects also practiced a form of mindfulness meditation, but the key to improvement was refuting negative thoughts. A full eight-week course of CBT resulted in significant clinical improvement in the people who completed the study. After the eight-week program, researchers followed patients for a year. Two out of three patients did not experience a relapse into depression. It was a significant result.

In 2002, Segal collaborated with Helen Mayberg to broaden the same study. This time they also conducted PET scans to see if the change of mind produced a shift in brain metabolism. It did. As in the study on OCD, treatment response was associated with significant metabolic changes in the brain. "In essence," Mayberg stated, "depression stems from a malfunction not in a single spot in the brain, but in a network or circuit of brain connections."[11] As patients practiced thinking differently, the network reset itself by turning down neural areas responsible for rumination and worry.

Thus, the answer to the question, *can the mind change the brain?*, is yes. The Dalai Lama was correct. In persistently posing this question, the Dalai Lama rested his case on a revered Tibetan teacher who once remarked: "One of the mind's most marvelous qualities is that it can be transformed."[12] I think it is safe to say that most of us would agree with this statement. Most of us have experienced a life-changing event that expanded our understanding and sense of self. We now know that a mind-expanding experience can light up dampened brain circuits, strengthen weak or faulty neural connections, and build new pathways to sustain greater happiness and competence. A fundamental shift in attitude produces neuronal changes that bring on the good life. If we are wired for stress, anxiety, or pessimism and want to change, we can rewire our brain by practicing a better thought for a happier feeling to sustain a positive attitude. When we do, our gray matter appears to turn into a veritable field of dreams. Build a field by practicing an experience you want to develop, and the neurons will come.

ONE OF THE MIND'S MOST MARVELOUS QUALITIES IS THAT IT CAN BE TRANSFORMED.

THE MYSTIC AND THE SCIENTIST

In challenging neuroscience to break from dogma and reconsider the mind–brain connection, the Dalai Lama served another purpose. He

brought psychology, spirituality, and neurology together in the same lab to investigate how a healthy mind generates a healthy brain to sustain the emotional, intellectual, and spiritual intelligence for a better life. To this end, the Dalai Lama and Richard Davidson, a groundbreaking researcher in affective neurology, partnered to open a window into the mystical brain. The Dalai Lama provided the mystics, and Davidson provided the lab.

Davidson is a professor at the University of Wisconsin and a fellow of the American Academy of Arts and Sciences. He pioneered a way of measuring an individual's mood set point by measuring brain activity in the prefrontal cortex. Davidson found that when the left prefrontal cortex sustained substantially higher activity than in the right, people reported feeling content, energetic, engaged, and joyful. They possessed a positive attitude, felt in control of life, and were enthusiastic about the future. They pursued personal growth and possessed an inner purpose. If life knocked them down, they were quick to rebound. In short, they had realized Aristotle's good life.

In contrast, when brain activity on the right side was dominant, people reported feeling anxious, stressed, depressed, and worried. Their attitude was negative. People whose right side activity was especially pronounced were likely candidates for clinical depression. Davidson was able to establish an index of the baseline activity between the right and left prefrontal cortex that can accurately predict our general attitude in everyday life. Davidson was interested to see what effect the intense mental training of Tibetan monks had on their left–right ratio. Did mental training shift the emotional dial from right to left and, if so, how far?

In 2001, Davidson tested a number of Tibetan monks who had devoted a substantial part of their lives to mindfulness meditation. These monks turned out to have the most extreme value to the left of anyone previously tested. Activity in the left prefrontal cortex (positive emotion) swamped activity in the right prefrontal cortex (negative emotions), something never before seen from purely mental activity.

The monks had much greater activation in brain regions called the right insula and caudate, a network that underlies empathy and maternal love. To assess the depth of empathy in monks, the researchers tested their ability to recognize fleeting facial expressions that indicate fear, anger, or disdain. The monks scored far higher than any one of the five thousand who have been tested. "They do better than policemen, lawyers, psychiatrists, customs officials, and judges," stated Dr. Paul Ekman of the University of California at San Francisco. Monks even did better than Secret Service agents, who previously had scored the highest.[13] They also had stronger connections from the frontal regions to the emotional regions, which is the pathway by which higher thought can control emotions.[14]

In addition, the monks showed a dramatically higher level of gamma wave activity involved in higher mental activity. Through mental training, these monks had developed the neural circuitry for a deeply peaceful, caring, and engaging intelligence that was completely positive in outlook. Even when the monks were not meditating, they sustained these optimal brain states.

During the monk study, Davidson taught a number of volunteers to meditate and then tested them. All were novices at meditation. "After a very small amount of meditation training," Davidson stated, "they showed a slight but significant increase in the gamma signal."

It's in Every One of Us

When Daniel Goleman asked the Dalai Lama what greater benefit he hoped for from this line of research, he replied:

Through training the mind, people can become more calm—especially those who suffer from too many ups and downs. That's the conclusion from these studies of Buddhist mind training. And that's my main end: I'm not thinking how to further Buddhism but how the Buddhist tradition can make some contribution to the benefit of society. Of course, as Buddhists, we always pray for all sentient beings. But we're only human beings; the main thing you can do is train your own mind.[15]

To test if this training was transferable to everyone, Davidson joined forces with Jon Kabat-Zinn of the University of Massachusetts in yet another study, focusing this time on stress in the workplace.[16] Kabat-Zinn is a pioneer in the emerging field of mind–body medicine. The study focused on stressed workers in a high-pressure biotech business. As part of the study, workers were trained in mindfulness meditation three hours a week for two months to see if meditation could shift attitudes, improve moods, and mitigate the high level of stress experienced by the workers. Davidson took readings of the prefrontal cortex of each of the workers, before and after the training. Before the mindfulness training, the readings on the workers' prefrontal cortex, on average, leaned to the right (negative emotion). After the eight-week training program, however, on average their readings shifted to the left, toward positive emotion. "Simultaneously, their moods improved; they reported feeling engaged again in their work, more energized, and less anxious."[17]

The evidence is that, within a defined practice, the mood set point can shift, and in a relatively short period of time. Davidson also reported that improved immune function accompanied the shift in attitude. Following a company-sponsored flu shot clinic, Davidson collected blood samples. He found higher quantities of flu antibodies in the bloodstream of those who had participated in the mindfulness program, compared to employees who had not. This meant that the immune systems of the people in the study were no longer dampened by stress.

WHAT DID THE MONKS DO?

Obviously, the next question to answer is: what did the monks practice to effect such positive changes in brain function?

The monks in the study evoked a number of inner states, or qualities, through a form of mindfulness meditation. One of the methods the monks chose to practice during the study is called one-pointedness. It is fully focused concentration on a single object of attention. This is the quality of a quiet, open-mindedness that allows you to be fully present with whatever you engage. We are not caught in the past or worried about the future, both of which are stressful states. We possess "a quiet sense of our own presence," as Eckhart Tolle wrote, "our own aliveness that flows into whatever we are doing."[18]

Here is an interesting proposition: we cannot be stressed when fully present. You, the reader, can approach the essence of this quiet, unattached way of being. It provides a refreshing break from life in the fast lane. Wherever you happen to be, simply become quiet inside, until you reach the point that you can feel your own breath. Allow yourself to be fully present. Look at your surroundings. Notice the objects, people, and colors that are present. See if you can feel the energy in the space. Consider the fact that now is the only time there is, and enjoy it. Allow your attention to settle on one object in your midst and give the object your full attention. Relax into the vibrancy and aliveness of attention. Of course, habitual thoughts, labels, judgments, and emotions will arise and string together, pulling you in another direction. Simply let these distractions come and go, and return to this quiet, alive focus of attention. When we miss this moment, we literally miss our life. Life almost always renews and refreshes us when we return to the present moment. Often, we can shift the stress in a demanding day simply by taking a moment's break to look out the window and catch a glimpse of the day outside. It can be quite soothing simply to observe the weather, or the dance of light and shadow at a particular time of day, or to watch the rain fall or the wind rustling through the trees.

Next, the monks evoked "a fearless certainty, a deep confidence that nothing can unsettle."[19] This is an attitude of calm. It means we are not afraid or threatened by what is happening on the outside. As a result, we can face challenges as they come. During the study, one monk was placed in an fMRI for three continuous hours. For some people, twenty minutes in that tube can feel like an eternity. When the procedure was over, this monk emerged joyful and energetic from the arduous process, proclaiming, "It's like a mini-retreat!"

Try this simple exercise: Think of a recent situation that you did not handle well. Imagine the same situation, but this time as you engage the situation, imagine that your attitude is peaceful rather than conflicted. How would you have behaved differently? Would you have been more open-minded, more tolerant? Would you have made fewer judgments? Could it have reduced the odds of making a mistake? How would you have felt at the conclusion of the encounter?

Another state the monks practiced was holding an attitude of loving kindness and compassion. This is the principle of relationship. It is leading with a sense of connection in whatever we do, first by connecting to our own internal center, then with others, and, at moments of solitude, with that which is greater than us. It is an unconditional, positive regard for others, strength-finding rather than fault-finding, forgiving instead of condemning, and valuing empathy over judgment.

Think of a person with whom you have had difficulty at home or at work. Think of two or three of their glaring faults. Notice how this feels. Now think of two or three positive qualities you can see in this person. Notice how this feels. Which one makes you feel more connected, not only to them but to your own heart? Which evokes a more peaceful attitude in you? The answer is obvious.

The monks also visualized the details of a *thangka*, a Tibetan wall painting depicting a deity. They mentally built the whole picture from top to bottom, until they arrived at a clear and complete mental image of it. This is the principle of relating to the whole of life instead of the fragments. It is seeing life as a process, not a destination, and the process as one of becoming rather than arriving. It is a state of growth rather than a fixed state, relating to ourselves not as grown but as growing; encompassing our failures and successes, our joys and sorrows, our positive qualities and those that are not so positive. The perfection lies in the imperfections. Viewing our life as whole involves an attitude of faith. It is faith in the journey we are undertaking. It is seeing a mistake as valuable because of what was learned. If we are seriously ill, wholeness is a process of getting well that includes living well with the time we have. Regardless of the situation, whenever we are able to meet ourselves in the present moment and open fully to our experience, the sense of wholeness gradually arises to form a clear and complete experience.

MYSTIC COOL

The mental states that the monks evoked during the study can be translated into four basic qualities for living, which anyone can practice and strengthen:

1. The first quality is *attention*. It is a way of being that is quietly engaged and fully present.

2. The second is our *inner stance*. It is the strength to remain calm and clear inside, regardless of what is happening outside.

3. The third quality is *extension*. It is the quality of our presence in all our relationships that sustains a sense of connection.

4. The fourth is *perspective*. It is an enduring sense of the whole that transcends the fragments.

When these elements merge into an attitude, their unity establishes a fearless self-confidence through which a person turns to face the world. This book gives this fearless self-confidence a name: Mystic Cool. Mystic Cool represents a form of mindfulness that integrates elements of humanistic and positive psychology with the psychospiritual approach called attitudinal healing.[20] These elements combine to attain and sustain a mindful shift in attitude, without relying on meditation exclusively to generate the shift. Mystic Cool is an approach we can all use, on our own, to shift habitually fearful, stressful reactions at the point of inception. It works in much the same way as Jeffrey Schwartz's approach to obsessive-compulsive disorder and Zindel Segal's approach to depression. Mystic Cool defines *peace* as power and *empowerment* as letting go of fear. Fear is the primary obstacle, and Mystic Cool serves to lift the mind from emotional distress and negativity to reach conscious choice. Through conscious choice, we can direct our actions toward the outcomes we desire. It is using our mind, instead of our mind using us. Mystic Cool focuses attention, establishes our inner stance, or attitude, and sustains the inner clarity and interpersonal resonance to reach the optimal experience of flow.

One of my greatest teachers on the power of peace was Mount Shasta. Mount Shasta is the second highest mountain in the continental United States. It is glacial and classified as a technical climb, meaning you need crampons, an ice ax, a hard hat, special clothing and boots, a subzero sleeping bag, and a long list of other essentials to undertake the journey. You also need to be in excellent physical condition. As in life, externals are not unimportant. The mountain is unforgiving of those who neglect even small details in preparing to make the climb. It can seem very complicated and daunting, but climbing Mount Shasta demands more than being tactically prepared. It requires an attitude of absolute simplicity and humility. This attitude can be absent in people who come to the mountain with the primary goal of "bagging" her. Hubris is lethal in mountain climbing. However, to a humble heart that surrenders to *Mis Misa*, the name native people have given her, the mountain becomes a guiding hand.

In the beginning, my mind was preoccupied with reaching my destination, which was the summit. After a few hours, this goal became blurred in weariness, and my focus shifted to more immediate locations. I began to fixate on small plateaus or crevices just ahead that promised a place of rest. These positions almost always turned out to be a mirage of shadow and light, which was discouraging.

The higher I climbed, the harder it got, and for the first couple hours, my mind complained incessantly about the hardship, undermining the positive attitude it takes to reach the top. It badgered me with: *What have I gotten myself into? What was I thinking when I decided to do this? It's crazy to go on. I can't make it. This mountain is going to kill me.* Eventually, I realized that my mind was making me miserable, depleting my physical and emotional energy. I realized I had to let go of reaching any destination at all. I had to stop thinking and begin disciplining myself to focus on the step I was taking, to be fully present in the moment and alive in the experience. It is as Eckhart Tolle stated in his book *The Power of Now*: "The moment you completely accept your nonpeace, your nonpeace becomes transmuted into peace."[21]

It took some time to master this orientation, but gradually I calmed down and eased into accepting whatever experience occupied a given moment, from dispiriting fatigue to expansive joy, from overwhelm to surrender. Then something I had not expected happened. My mind began to quiet, and as it quieted I suddenly woke up to the experience I was having. The beauty of the mountain lifted my heart and expanded my mind as I watched the shadows of billowy clouds race across the undulating contour, darkening its surface, and then restoring it to pure white as they sailed by. I became aware that I was literally walking in other people's footprints, etched in the ice, making the way easier to find, and I was bolstered by the courage of those who had preceded me. My heart opened wide to the people I was climbing with. They became brothers and sisters to me. I was touched by the way we watched out for each other, slowed the pace at times to let someone catch up, and how we quietly celebrated each other's courage to continue to venture higher.

Gradually, effort transformed into flow, and within this feeling of flow I was carried along by a force or presence of something greater than I was. It was nothing less than miraculous. I had no sense of time or even a sense of self. The mountain and I were at peace and at one with each other, without a shred of ego or conflict to separate us. That year I made it to the summit, weathering fifty-mile-an-hour winds through the corridor leading to the top. I had reached what felt like the top of the world. I knew, though, it was not ice, altitude, forty-degree snowfields, and fifty-mile-an-hour winds that I had conquered in reaching the summit. It was my fear I had conquered. When I engaged the present moment quietly, attentively, sensually, the strength of what I am came alive. When I remained calm inside, regardless of the difficulty, clarity emerged to point the way. When I connected with my heart and to others, through appreciation, a force greater than I was carried me. When I remained open to my experience, without judging it, my sense of self as a whole naturally arose.

IT WAS NOT ICE, ALTITUDE, FORTY-DEGREE SNOWFIELDS,
AND FIFTY-MILE-AN-HOUR WINDS THAT
I HAD CONQUERED IN REACHING THE SUMMIT.
IT WAS MY FEAR I HAD CONQUERED.

THE HIGHEST QUALITY OF LIFE IS PEACE

The highest quality of life is peace and the joy it generates. Peace facilitates the full use of our powers toward achieving excellence. This is the definition of Mystic Cool. The four qualities of Mystic Cool are not new to most of us. We have learned them through the trial and error of living, and we appreciate their worth. The problem comes because we do not apply them consistently or completely enough to change the experience of our everyday lives. The next section of the book is designed to help us reassimilate these values.

The summit we seek is peace; it is the joy in our journey. It is the intrinsic reward to be found in a state of flow, reaching for excellence. Peace brings a deeper appreciation for who and what we are, extending the same appreciation to others. It offers an enthusiastic faith in what we can accomplish through a change of mind. Peace is the threshold to everything we view as intelligence. It facilitates the capacity to formulate our attitude, focus our attention, plan and problem solve, love, create, and synthesize heart, head, and emotion into noetic power. It is the mystery of divinity incarnate, which is two winged dragons drawing the chariot of Mars that carries Apollo.

In the depths of winter, I finally learned
there was in me an invincible summer.

Albert Camus

Achieving this beautiful mind requires an inwardly calming presence to quiet Mars. Thus, the shift we need to make is the psychological shift from fear to peace—from debilitating emotion and stress to a dynamic state of calm. The more we walk in mindfulness, the more we take charge of brain and mind, the wider the possibilities. There are virtually no limits to what we can do if we put our right mind to it. "The difference between what we do and what we are capable of doing," stated Mahatma Gandhi, "would suffice to solve most of the world's problems."

Four Qualities, Three Steps

Each of the four qualities of Mystic Cool represents an essential shift from fear to peace. There are three steps we can take to master these four qualities.

1. The first step is awareness. *Awareness* relaxes stressful patterns and opens the door to choice.

2. The second step is practice. *Practice* defines specific choices implicit within the four qualities of Mystic Cool. As we consistently make theses choices, we strengthen neural connections that support higher brain function for optimal experience. Eventually, a consistent practice will wire our brain for the joyful calm that is the foundation for a good life.

3. The third step is *extension*. It is extending to others the internal shift we have mastered that generates positive, constructive, and meaningful relationships.

It's Just Around the Corner

There are scientists who believe that nature must take another step in the evolution of the human brain. They believe we require a neural bridge to more a sustainable, higher, and humane consciousness. Robert Jastrow of Columbia University thinks that "in the next stage of evolution after man, we can expect that a still newer and greater brain will join the 'old' to work in concert with the neocortex in directing the behavior of a form of life as superior to man as he is to the ancient forest mammal."[22] What a wonderful leap that would be! Yet, even small evolutionary changes take as much as twenty-five thousand years to accomplish. Humanity does not appear to have that kind of time. There are those of us don't have twenty-five years. We cannot wait for nature, and it seems nature cannot wait for us. Our problems, globally and personally, need solutions now.

The question that defines our challenge is this: can our state of consciousness evolve to begin to change our brains in the next one hundred days? The answer, gleaned from research, is yes. With mindfulness, we can. The Tibetan monks have proved that our innate neural architecture can be shaped to produce an infinitely humane intelligence, but only if we genuinely want it. Even a small amount of practice goes a long way, as demonstrated in the research on people who suffered from depression and obsessive-compulsive disorder. From this point forward, we will be looking at approaches that can end the internal conflict that makes life stressful and unfulfilling, and sometimes leads people to be destructive. We will be working with approaches that can shift our attitude, raise our consciousness, and rewire our brain, making the shift easier and easier to sustain. The good life is just around the corner, and turning that corner is simpler than you might think.

6
Awareness: The Storm

To become the spectator of one's own life . . .
is to escape the suffering of life.

Oscar Wilde

A wareness is the first step in building the attitude that can rewire
our brain to deliver the good life. There is a remarkable power in
awareness. We can transcend much of the stress that plagues us simply
by bringing our patterns of distress into the light of day. Awareness
enables us to see through the illusions fear produces. Initially, most of
my clients find it hard to believe that simply witnessing, nonjudgmentally, the thoughts, emotions, and sensations in a pattern of stress could
resolve much of the problem. Then they try it and within two weeks are
amazed at the difference it has made. One client, who was ten days into
the process, told me she was walking down a hall at work and realized
that she felt "quietly joyful inside" and "definitely at ease." "And for no
apparent reason," she added. There was a reason for her state of mind,
however. Awareness had routinely collapsed negative, stress-provoking
thoughts that previously had strung together and proliferated into
emotional upheavals, causing perceptions of threats where no real
threat existed.

If you can just observe what you are and move with it,
then you will find that it is possible to go infinitely far.

J. Krishnamurti

Bringing these patterns into the light is the single most important step we can take. Recall the studies on obsessive-compulsion disorder and clinical depression presented in chapter 5. By bringing negative tendencies into awareness, patients with OCD were able to refute obsessive thoughts and compulsions. Patients with depression were able to break the tendency to ruminate, misperceive, and view situations as catastrophes.

We cannot change a condition we do not understand. Awareness increases understanding, understanding empowers choice, and choice moves us in a new direction. The symptoms that mark OCD, anxiety disorders, and clinical depression are extreme versions of symptoms a teacher, parent, or executive suffers when chronically under stress. Often people are not aware of the degree to which they are stressed. We get worked up over a traffic jam that threatens to make us late for an appointment. Two hours later, we quake with frustration when our computer freezes. In the afternoon, we snap at a colleague for the crime of interrupting us with a question. On the ride home, our mind obsesses over small details that do not seem quite perfect. In the middle of the night, we wake up worried and pace the floor. We tend to dismiss these reactions as just another irritating day in the modern world, instead of as manifestations of an unhealthy brain driven by an unhealthy mind.

In an article titled "Building Up to a Meltdown," the *Los Angeles Times* reported on a fifty-two-year-old, high-level executive for a large computer manufacturer, who was a self-described workaholic. He believed he was effectively managing the daily demands and pressures until, late one night, he woke up with tightness in his chest, barely able to breathe. His doctor diagnosed an anxiety attack caused by stress and told him to slow down. "I didn't know what stress was," the executive stated, "I didn't think I had stress."[1] This account is not uncommon. Stress reactions can fall below our radar. We can become desensitized to the havoc stress makes of our minds and the symptoms it is causing in our body. As we have seen, we pay a heavy price cognitively, emotionally, and physically, when unconscious reactions become a chronic feature in our lives.

Don Joseph Goewey

Out of the Storm, Into the Eye

In this chapter, we are going to deconstruct the storm called stress, bringing its many faces into greater awareness. We will look at stress, up close and personal, to help us identify our individual stress pattern—or our stress fingerprint. In the chapter that follows, we are going to penetrate the eye of the storm. The eye is the dynamic place of peace and joy to which the Greeks pointed. It is the place where we attain our absolute best. It is the good life. A mind under stress tends to think of the eye as a faraway shore on the other side of a turbulent sea. It can feel so far away that we doubt its existence. The eye is nearer than we think, and it was not that long ago that we landed on that bright shore and spent a day in its glorious calm. The question is not: does it exist? The real question is: how do we reach that shore every day and stay all day long? Awareness is a big part of the answer.

The first fact we need to clarify for ourselves is that stress is internal. Often, we confuse the source of stress as objective rather than subjective. A mind under stress tends to perceive stress as emanating from outside events. Stress is happening in us far more than it is happening to us. Our mind is quite capable of generating all sorts of stressful events solely in our heads. When we are in a stress reaction, we are prone to perceive negative emotions as facts and hold someone or something responsible for the upset. A mind under stress tends to believe people or events caused our distress, not our own thoughts, feelings, and attitudes. Thus, a mind under stress is prone to feel victimized, pointing a finger and blaming outside forces for the way we feel inside.

In trainings I conduct, people sometimes resist the idea that stress is internal, challenging me to walk a mile in their shoes. Subordinates point to the stress of dealing with an explosive boss, managers point to the aggravation of coping with an intractable employee, and parents cite an incorrigible teenager. Some people even feel condemned by the idea, as if it shifts the "blame" for a stressful life to them. In the workshop, I take participants through an exercise in which I ask them to list the elements that are present when they feel particularly stressed.

I stand at the easel, capturing the one-word answers participants toss up to describe their experience of stress. Without fail, internal factors account for no less than 80 percent of what people list at every workshop. Here is the list from the last workshop:

Anxiety	Sleeplessness	My Team
Confusion	Teenager	Discouraged
Conflict	Changes	Defeated
Anger	Spaced Out	Meetings
Defensive	Expectations	Family Demands
Loss of Focus	Depressed	Fear of Failure
Withdrawn	Traffic Jams	To-Do List
Loss of Control	Stuck	Poor Memory
Overwhelm	My Boss	Scattered

When it comes to people reflecting on the origin of stress, internal states trump the red ink at the bottom of the balance sheet or the memo that announces plans to downsize. People even define seemingly external factors, such as traffic jams, bosses, or family demands, as exacerbated by our own internal reactions. At the conclusion of the exercise, I present people with the definition of stress formulated by Richard Lazarus, the eminent stress researcher from the University of California at Berkeley. Lazarus makes a clear distinction between *stress* and *stressors*. He defines a stressor as any kind of a demand, stating that these are relative in nature. One kind of stressor may be enervating for one person and energizing to another. Stress, on the other hand, is an appraisal that something must be done, along with the perception that the demand will overwhelm our resources. In other words, becoming reactive or constructively engaged with whatever demand life makes ultimately hinges on our internal response.

The more we are able to experience the patterns that overwhelm and confine us, the more visible they become. The more visible they become, the easier they are to shift.

A Scientific Definition of Stress

Stressor

• Any kind of demand or change

Stress

• The appraisal that something must be done about the stressor, along with the perception that the demand overwhelms our resources

---

SOME GUIDELINES FOR MAKING THE SHIFT

In the section that follows, we have the opportunity to increase our awareness of stress in our daily life. The key is a willingness to allow the thoughts, feelings, sensations, and attitudes driving our stress reactions to surface. This entails being mindful not to judge or condemn our reactions or ourselves. It involves embracing the exercises we will do, staying with the discomfort it may cause and meeting it with an attitude of curiosity. As odd as it may sound, it also entails letting go of the need for anything to change or to be otherwise, and accepting what emerges exactly as it is, even negativity and irrationality. It means having compassion for the way fear conditioning wired our brain for stress, and being patient with the process that rewires it for peace. There is an old theory in psychology that says the way a person handles one thing is the way he handles everything. Often, deconstructing one stressful event can give the basic pattern that is activated whenever we are stressed. It's like the guy who declares, *there's only one fear in life*, and when asked what it is says, *I don't know. I'm too afraid to look.*

GUIDED IMAGERY

We're going to take a look at stress using guided imagery. By *guided imagery*, I am referring to a technique in which people use imagination to visualize an event or outcome. Guided imagery is an effective approach to identifying internal patterns often outside of awareness. It can be highly effective in easing stress, promoting an attitude of peace and reframing a self-defeating mindset. The research on guided imagery has demonstrated significant results in reducing hospital stays, alleviating pain, and resolving post-traumatic stress.[2] Studies have even shown that guided imagery can affect disease outcome, which is why it is utilized in a number of oncology centers.

Initially, people can be resistant to guided processes, but there is much to be gained by jumping in with both feet and using this powerful tool. Jack Nicklaus attributed much of his performance to the visualization process. "I never hit a shot," Nicklaus said, "not even in practice, without having a very sharp, in-focus picture of it in my head. First I see the ball where I want it to finish, nice and white and sitting up high on the bright green grass. Then the scene quickly changes, and I see the ball going there; its path, trajectory, and shape, even its behavior on landing. Then there is a sort of fade-out, and the next scene shows me making the kind of swing that will turn the previous images into reality."[3]

Mihaly Csikszentmihalyi describes a prisoner of war who was placed in solitary confinement in Vietnam.[4] To maintain his sanity, every day he played a mental game of golf on his home course. He visualized every aspect of the game, including walking the steps between shots. Upon his release, he returned home and although physically compromised by the ordeal of captivity, on his first time back out on the course he shot the best game of his life.

WHAT'S STRESSING ME?[5]

The first step to take in building awareness is to identify three current situations or areas of our life that have been particularly stressful. The purpose of this exercise is to identify undercurrents and patterns of stress that are usually subliminal. Take out a piece of paper and follow the instructions below.

1. Reflect on three recent situations in which you felt stressed. Keep it current. Draw from the last week or month.

2. On your sheet of paper, describe each situation separately. Casually capture the basic elements of each situation.

3. When you have completed the task, choose the one that has the most intensity for you. Place a check next to it.

Taking It Deeper

Now focus on the stressful situation that has the most intensity for you. Use the following steps to visualize it. Read what follows all the way through first and then mentally take yourself through the steps.

1. Close your eyes for a moment and remember the stressful event.

2. Make this situation real by remembering where you were when it occurred. Make it vivid. Imagine it as if it were happening now.

3. See your surroundings. Where are you? Is it morning, afternoon, or night?

4. Did the situation involve another person? If so, see his or her face.

5. Notice what you are thinking as you relate to this situation.

6. Notice your emotions. Are you angry? Frightened? Overwhelmed? Depressed?

7. Notice what is happening in your body. Is your heart beating quickly? Are you sweating? Are you shaky? Do you feel a tightening in your back or neck?

8. For a few moments, remain in this stressful state until the feeling of it is vivid.

9. What is your attitude at the end of the encounter? Is it positive or negative? Are you optimistic or pessimistic?

10. When you sense you are finished, open your eyes and take two or three slow breaths.

APPLYING THE STRESSOMETER[6]

The second step we can take in building awareness is to deconstruct our pattern of stress in terms of its mental, emotional, physical, and attitudinal impact. The Stressometer below can be used to graphi-

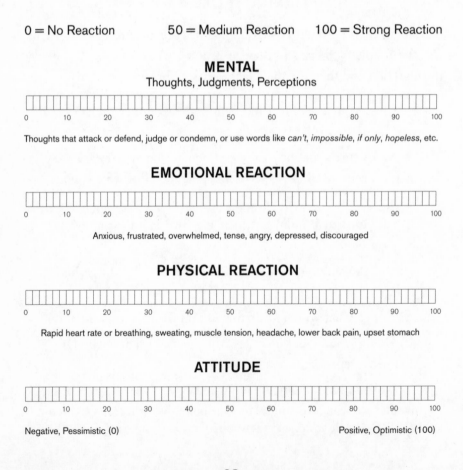

0 = No Reaction   50 = Medium Reaction   100 = Strong Reaction

MENTAL
Thoughts, Judgments, Perceptions

0   10   20   30   40   50   60   70   80   90   100

Thoughts that attack or defend, judge or condemn, or use words like *can't*, *impossible*, *if only*, *hopeless*, etc.

EMOTIONAL REACTION

0   10   20   30   40   50   60   70   80   90   100

Anxious, frustrated, overwhelmed, tense, angry, depressed, discouraged

PHYSICAL REACTION

0   10   20   30   40   50   60   70   80   90   100

Rapid heart rate or breathing, sweating, muscle tension, headache, lower back pain, upset stomach

ATTITUDE

0   10   20   30   40   50   60   70   80   90   100

Negative, Pessimistic (0)   Positive, Optimistic (100)

cally chart your level or reactivity in these four areas on a scale of 0 to 100. Zero equates to no reaction, while 100 equates to a strong reaction.

An alternate approach: if you have difficulty determining a value, simply use your imagination. What number between 0 and 100 pops into your head as you view each area presented in the Stressometer? Don't argue with it. Don't analyze it. Mentally capture the number and then draw a line on the graph to the point that matches it.

RECOGNIZING THE PATTERN

When you are finished, look at the graphs.

Which area is the most intense, which is next, and so on?

Is this a typical pattern for you when you are under stress?

Now refer back to the page titled "What's Stressing Me" (page 90).

Does the same pattern apply to the other two stressful situations that you listed?

IDENTIFYING THE SIGNS OF STRESS[7]

The third step in building awareness is identifying your specific symptoms of stress. The following worksheet helps you do this.

Signs of Stress: Part 1 is a checklist of physical, emotional, and cognitive symptoms

Signs of Stress: Part 2 is a checklist of spiritual, relational, and behavioral symptoms

Check any symptom that you experience to any degree. Don't be concerned if you think the symptom is stress related or not. If you experience it, check it.

After you have finished, review the items you checked.

SIGNS OF STRESS – PART I

PHYSICAL	EMOTIONAL	COGNITIVE
☐ Racing Heart	☐ Unhappy	☐ Attention Deficit
☐ Dry Mouth	☐ Angry	☐ Memory Lapses
☐ Upset Stomach	☐ Frustrated	☐ Incessant Thought
☐ Diarrhea	☐ Troubled Sleep	☐ Pessimistic
☐ Gas, Belching	☐ Sleepless	☐ Disorganized
☐ Rashes	☐ Depressed	☐ Blocked
☐ Muscle Tension	☐ Unmotivated	☐ Fragmented
☐ Headache	☐ Nervous	☐ Indecisive
☐ Hyperventilation	☐ Anxious	☐ Distracted
☐ Frequent Sighing	☐ Overreactive	
☐ Sweating	☐ Hopeless	
☐ Appetite Change	☐ Volatile	
☐ Frequent Colds, Flu	☐ Paranoid	
☐ Fatigue		

SIGNS OF STRESS – PART II

SPIRITUAL	RELATIONAL	BEHAVIORAL
☐ Emptiness	☐ Feel Separate	☐ Smoking
☐ Self-doubt	☐ Resentment	☐ Alcohol/Drug Use
☐ Loss of Meaning	☐ Attack/Defend	☐ Overeating
☐ Apathy	☐ Untrusting	☐ Not Eating
☐ Unforgiving	☐ Fault-Finder	☐ Poor Diet Choices
☐ Disconnected	☐ Fault-Finding	☐ Skipping Exercise
☐ Muscle Tension	☐ Unmotivated	☐ Road Rage
☐ Cynical	☐ Lonely	
☐ Lack of Peace	☐ Anxious	
☐ No Vacation	☐ No Time for Friends	
☐ Skip Holidays	☐ Miss Family Events	

1. Identify any that tend to be more intense than others and place a star next to them.

2. Identify those that you have tried to change but have not succeeded in doing so. Place a check mark next to them.

3. Were there any surprises in reviewing the Signs of Stress? Were there signs that, before the exercise, you had not equated with stress? If so, circle them.

4. What did you find in the Signs of Stress that you did not remember or experience during the visualization we did in the What's Stressing Me exercise? Was this sign active during that stressful event?

5. Carefully examine all the information in What's Stressing Me, the Stressometer, and Signs of Stress exercises until you begin to see a pattern.

THE TELL

The information you have now gathered from these three simple exercises is your tell. In poker, a tell is the way an unconscious change in a player's behavior or emotional state telegraphs his reaction to the cards he holds. He may lean forward, fidget, make facial expressions, start to sweat, or sigh heavily. In essence, the person exhibiting a tell is unconsciously revealing signs of stress. One factor that distinguishes a master poker player is a keen awareness of every sign, symptom, and gesture of stressful reactions in other people. They learn this skill from dissecting their own tell. Over the course of a poker game, these masters carefully track another player's tell and use it to great advantage.

You gain an advantage over your own habitual stress reactions if you bring your tell into awareness. Reviewing the knowledge you have just acquired about your tell is a good beginning. Applying what you have learned in real situations will deepen your understanding of the pattern. Gradually, bringing your stress pattern into greater awareness frees you to respond to adversity with peace instead of fear, with calm instead of conflict.

Here is a classic example of how a stress tell can work with conscious choice to dissolve a stress reaction. Imagine working hard for several days to complete a project that you just finished and submitted to the boss. You feel good about your work and are hopeful the boss will be pleased. The next morning, on the way to your office, you see the boss approaching from the opposite direction. His expression is fixed, his lips are pursed, and his attitude seems stern. As he comes near, you smile pleasantly and extend a cheerful good morning. He walks by without returning the greeting or making eye contact.

Your heart thumps and your gaze turns downward. Your mind seeks an explanation for the boss's behavior and soon fills with worried, fearful thoughts that assume the worst. As you walk to your office, you distractedly wipe beads of sweat from your forehead. By the time you reach your desk, you're angry, thinking: *All the hours I logged putting that project together. The time I took away from my family to finish on time.* A half hour later, a colleague arrives for a meeting, but you are distracted and can hardly focus on what she says. At the end of the meeting, your colleague departs thinking the same thoughts about you that you are having about the boss.

These are the debilitating signs and symptoms of a stress reaction. If, however, you have worked at deconstructing your stress pattern to identify your tell, you will be conscious of the thump in your chest. It is now familiar to you. You might even identify the thump as a burst of adrenaline entering your bloodstream, signaling the first signs of fight-or-flight. Catching this, you are able to recognize your first fearful thoughts and to remember how quickly stressful thinking can ignite a stress reaction in you. You are able to recognize that you have a choice. You pause for a moment, acknowledging that you do not know what the boss's behavior means and that it is hardly worth a stress reaction. You take a deep breath and choose to let go of the incident.

FEEL IT TO HEAL IT

The fourth step in building awareness can actually be surprisingly therapeutic. It can relieve tension. The purpose of the next exercise is to demonstrate how the awareness of physical manifestations of stress can be used as a tool to shift out of stress. This exercise can be used every day to relieve the tension in the body that stress causes. It requires four minutes to perform. You can do it at your desk at work, or in bed if you are having trouble falling asleep. The effect is astonishing. It is called "Feel It to Heal It." Read it through first and then mentally go through the steps.

1. Close your eyes.

2   Allow yourself to feel your body.

3. Notice stress in an area that is particularly uncomfortable.

4. Feel the discomfort, tightness, or tension there.

5. Now scan your body for tension or discomfort in another place. Feel it.

6. Scan for another area of discomfort. Feel it.

7. Keep scanning for other areas of discomfort and repeat the process of feeling the discomfort.

8. Now see if you can feel your body as a whole. How does your whole body feel?

9. Imagine for a moment that your body is neutral and that there is an emotional body that can be felt or intuited through the physical body.

10. What is your emotional state at the moment? Feel it without imposing any judgment, letting go of the tendency to want to change it. Simply feel how it feels with curiosity.

11. Gradually allow yourself to relax into the feeling. Let the sensation come to the surface. Simply be with whatever you feel.

12. Take two easy breaths and let go of the emotion.

13. On the next breath, feel the sensation of air passing through your nostrils. Put your fingertips together very gently and feel the sensation of it. Release your fingers and feel other parts of your body, from your head to your toes. Feel the tingling energy that is alive and active in each part.

14. Feel the inner body of energy radiating outward.

15. When you are ready, open your eyes. Look around the room, and take in the colors and shapes of what you see.

16. Be present in a fresh, alert way.

17. Embrace this moment as new, and relax. Feel the aliveness that is inherent in simple awareness.

CAPTURING THE FEELING

Take out a piece of paper and format it by drawing a line vertically down the full length of the paper, about two inches in from the right. At the top of the right column, write *Rating*. Above the left column, write *Areas of My Body*. Then write down areas that felt stressed and tense. Rate each according to level of discomfort, on a scale of 1 to 5, with 1 representing mild tension and 5 representing very tense.

Did the discomfort change as you felt it? What was the dominant feeling you experienced in the emotional body? Did your emotional state change at the end of the exercise as you became more fully present? In what way?

IF WE FIND OURSELVES IN A STRESS REACTION,
BY DEFINITION WE ARE EXPERIENCING
SOME FORM OF FEAR.

This guided process provides information about the stress carried in our bodies. Some people fear that allowing the physical tension and pain to surface will exacerbate it. The experience is quite the opposite for most people who do this exercise. It relieves tension and discomfort. The exercise can also bring to awareness the repressed emotion behind the tension, allowing the emotion to be experience and released. As we open to our experience, we gain an increasing trust in our total organism. Trusting how it is gravitates towards a more peaceful and therefore more satisfying experience of life, even if how it is distresses us at the moment. It is the difference between being tight and beginning to relax; between shutting down and feeling open, curious, and accepting of what occurs, moment to moment. Trusting our organism means we are alive in our experience instead of rejecting it or feeling negated and depleted by it.

GETTING TO THE SOURCE

The last, and perhaps most important, process in building awareness takes us to the source of a stress reaction—to the fearful thought process driving it. We have already established that stress and fear are biologically linked. Fear is the trigger that fires a stress reaction. Thus, we can dissolve a stress reaction by asking a simple question whenever we are under stress. That question is: what am I afraid of? We are going to do an exercise that will enable you to detect the fear beneath the most stressful situation you identified in the What's Stressing Me exercise.

I once conducted this exercise one-on-one with a prominent corporate lawyer who attended a training I presented. (I will call him Andrew.) Andrew was in litigation with another attorney representing a large corporation. He perceived his opponent as unethical, using words like *crook* and *shyster* to describe him. The opposing lawyer infuriated him, and Andrew was taking it home. He thought about it incessantly, lost sleep over it, and bored his wife with the base details at dinner. His wife was growing weary of hearing about it. As his stress level increased, Andrew began to lose his edge and make bad decisions. He came to the training desperate for techniques that could shift the situation to restore his power and allow him to pummel his adversary. I asked him, "In this situation, what are you afraid of?" *Losing*, was his answer.

What are you afraid of if you lose the case? I asked. *Looking like a fool*, he said with effect.

What's the fear of looking like a fool? *That I will lose my reputation.*
What's the fear in losing your reputation? *Losing my clients.*
What's the fear in losing clients? *Being asked to leave the firm.*

And what's the fear under this? *That I will end up pushing a shopping cart down Main Street.*

We then delved into each of his fearful thoughts, as you will see in a moment, and found that each one was an illusion. Not one was true. They were all lies fear was telling him, and he believed them. Believing made these fearful thoughts seem real, as if they were facts instead of just emotionally charged thoughts.

Part 1: What Am I Afraid Of? The Question that Turns Stress Around[8]

1. Bring to mind the stressful situation you have been investigating from the What's Stressing Me exercise.

2. Tune into this stressful situation once more. Experience it again.

3. Next, turn to the example on the following page, titled "What Am I Afraid Of?" and recreate the chart on a piece of paper.

4. Now ask yourself: in this stressful situation, what am I afraid of?

5. When you have your answer, write it down in the left column, keeping it to one sentence or a phrase.

6. Next, reference back to the previously stated fear, asking yourself: what am I afraid of if this happens? For example: Your first fear is *I am afraid that people are judging me unfairly.* In that case, the next question would be phrased: if people judge me unfairly, what I am afraid of? Write it down in one sentence or a phrase.

7. Repeat the process until you have identified five fears or until you feel complete.

Part 2: Refuting Fear with Reality

The next step is to inquire if there is any basis to these fears.

1. Turn to the first fear on your list. One by one, inquire into each of your answers to the question: what am I afraid of?

2. Ask yourself: Am I 100 percent certain that this thought is true? Not in part, but 100 percent?

3. If not, refute it with a more realistic statement. Let's take the example of the lawyer. Here is how his worksheet might look.

WHAT AM I AFRAID OF?	THE FEAR REFUTED
Losing the case	I have not lost the case yet. There is still a chance to win.
Looking like a fool	I am not a fool.
Losing my reputation	I am a respected litigator in this county.
Being asked to leave the firm	They are planning to make me a partner.
That I will end up pushing a shopping cart down Main Street	I have always made plenty of money.

Once you have refuted the fears on your list, ask yourself: who would I be without these fearful thoughts? Write down your answer on a separate piece of paper. Post what you just wrote where you will see it periodically over the next week.

At this point in the exercise, I usually read each column back to the client or workshop participant, turning it into a story. In the case of the lawyer, the fearful story would read like this: *I am losing the case, looking like a fool, and in the process I am losing my reputation, my job, and my livelihood. Next time you see me, I'll be pushing a shopping cart down Main Street with the few possessions I have left piled inside.*

Often, as I read participants their fear statements, they laugh. Some of the answers are hilarious. Of course, what is not funny is the brutal way this storyline operates unconsciously, behind the scenes. The flashes of fearful images and negative self-talk erode every ounce of confidence and optimism. When I bring the storyline into awareness and ask if it's true, the answer is always no. It is an illusion, a byproduct of fear. When I take people to the very bottom of their list of fearful outcomes, whatever the circumstance, the image most see is dying, disgraced, and unloved. This is what Mars, the emotional brain, sees and defends against—a threatening world bent on destroying us. And the point is that the greater part of it is mind-made.

Next I read them the storyline in the Fear Refuted column, which is closer to fact. In the case of the lawyer, the more realistic story would read like this: *I have not lost anything yet. Actually I could win (especially if I have a change of attitude). I have earned people's respect, my firm wants to promote me, and I am making good money.* When I ask participants if the refuted storyline is a truer statement about their current situation, the answer is always yes. Finally, I ask which of the statements they chose to believe when they were afraid and under stress. It can be quite an *ah-ha* to realize that there was a fundamental choice being made. The fearful choice was being made by an unfortunate wiring of the brain. When I ask: who would you be without these fearful thoughts, the answer is: at peace with a more optimistic outlook.

Transcending the Background of Negativity

The What Am I Afraid Of? exercise is intended to bring attention to the pattern of negative thoughts, feelings, and perceptions that are running automatically in the background, determining our experience and limiting our potential. It literally creates our reality. As we have just seen, these thoughts and reactions tell lies we are prone to believe and act upon. We have to wake up to get free of it. Awareness is the way we break the negative, reactive patterns. It is how we find fear's autopilot and turn it off. In his book *Awareness*, Anthony de Mello, the Jesuit priest known throughout the world for his writings and teaching, offers yet another way of dissolving reactive patterns through awareness.[9] It is a simple four-step process de Mello encourages us to practice every day, all day long over two weeks, starting today. Two weeks of vigilantly listening to negative thoughts and reactions may sound like a daunting task. It may seem so at first, but soon the rewards outweigh the initial discomfort. The more we persist the more we will see the delusion in our thinking and perceiving. Stress is the result of believing the distortions our delusional thinking generates.

As we practice de Mello's method below, we grasp a simple, obvious fact that eludes a stressful mind: we can choose not to believe our own negativity. Negative thoughts and reaction will no longer exercise power over our experience. It is wonderfully liberating. As de Mello stated, "I'll promise you this: I have not known a single person who gave time to being aware who didn't see a difference in a matter of weeks."

> **A thought is harmless unless we believe it.**
> **Byron Katie**

1. **Be aware of negative feelings and thoughts happening in you.** The first thing we need to do is get in touch with negative thoughts and feelings that occur outside of awareness—nervousness, tension, the sense that life is meaningless, anger, hatred, self-contempt, or some version of the thought that we are worthless. Small and large judgments also count, such as *he's a jerk, she has it in for me, that's stupid, or I don't like it.* Often, negativity begins in very subtle ways, such as a complaint that produces a slight wave of anxiety, or depression we fail to notice until it has saturated our mood. We don't understand it as the very stuff that is producing a background mental state of stress, anxiety, and unhappiness. Start noticing every aspect of it, without making judgments, analyzing it, or condemning yourself for having such thoughts or feelings. Let go of the need for it to change and simply notice it. Let the thought or feeling come into awareness.

2. **Understand that these negative feelings and thoughts are in you, not in reality.** Thoughts are not reality and emotions are not facts. Yet at times, especially when we are upset, we react as if what we think or feel is fact instead of speculation, truth instead of perception. A brain under stress is capable of generating sixty thousand negative, fearful, stress-provoking thoughts on a bad

day. When we believe fear's "text messages," we suffer terribly and often behave badly. The cure is to practice bringing stressful, fearful, negative thoughts into awareness and then neutralizing each one by not believing it. As we practice, we discover that a stressful thought is harmless if we do not believe in it. When we practice this every day, all day long, we erode the very structure that holds stress and suffering in place. The reward for mastering this simple shift is a mind free of stress. It is a mind dynamically at peace, cultivating an enthusiastic heart that opens the way to joy. It is *you* excelling at living.

3. **Do not identify with the negative feelings.** Although these feelings are *in* you, they are not *you*. The essential you is to the mind's negativity what the sky is to clouds. Let these negative thoughts and feelings pass like clouds across the sky. If I say, "I am angry," *I* is not the feeling. Anger is there and I am what is conscious of it. I am aware of the emotion. When we do not identify with anger but simply recognize it, anger glides on by. Anxiety passes. Disappointment dissolves.

4. **When you change, everything changes.** The last step tends to happen on its own as you begin to understand how thoughts, feelings, and attitudes determine what you see and experience in the world. "Awareness," wrote de Mello, "releases reality to change you." After a while, you don't have to make any effort because, as illusions begin to crumble, you begin to know genuine happiness.[10]

> ... negativity cannot contain our essentially positive nature,
> any more than what is small can contain what is vast.
> **Bronwyn Falcona**

Through this process, we begin to see, one by one, the negative thoughts we think and the painful feelings they produce in us. We begin to see the way they chain together to form an illusion that belief ordains as real. Much of what we call human suffering happens in this way. The cure is awareness. I have witnessed the same benefit in people I have worked with over the years. It is astonishing that something so simple could work so effectively on something as complicated as human suffering. But choosing not to believe an illusion that generates pain does work. It is not only simple, it is easy. The universe designed salvation to be mercifully simple. There is a poignant passage in *A Course in Miracles* that states:

> *Complexity is nothing but a screen of smoke, which hides the very simple fact that no decision can be difficult. What is the gain to you in learning this? It is far more than merely letting you make choices easily and without pain. Heaven itself is reached with empty hands and open minds, which come with nothing to find everything and claim it as their own.*[11]

In the next chapter, we will attempt to reach this free and easy state of mind that gives us everything. We have just met its first condition, which is to lay aside all of fear's self-deception. The second condition is learning to distinguish between that which gives us everything and that which promises everything but gives nothing.

7

The Eye of the Storm

Whoever I am, or whatever I am doing,
some kind of excellence is within my reach.

John W. Gardner

There is another experience we are capable of generating that is the polar opposite of a mind in fear and a brain under stress. It is the peace of mind and the joy of living that enables us to excel. To live this experience, we need to make our way to the eye of the storm. At the beginning of the previous chapter, I stated that the eye is nearer than we think. In fact, we pass through it all the time. The problem is we have not found a way to stay in the eye to make it our everyday experience. We can do it, however. Joy and peace are an essential part of our nature. We can learn to cultivate both by deconstructing those times when we slipped past the storm to stand in the bright light of the eye.

Take a few moments and reflect on the last time you felt at the top of your game. It was a time when a flow of intelligence took over and swept you along. You were in the zone. Time stood still, your mind cleared, and you worked with precision. You were able to focus your energy and attention, and minimize outside distractions. Pieces fell effortlessly into place, as if the dots were connecting themselves. Working in this way did not feel like work at all to you; instead it was a labor of love.

Now take out a piece of paper and do the following exercise:

1. At the top of the paper, write *My Experience When I Was at the Top of My Game.*

2. Make a list of inner qualities you experienced when you were at the top of your game, in the zone, and making things happen.

3. Use short phrases to capture your experience when you are in the Zone. Make a list of at least ten.

As we shall see later in this chapter, the qualities you experience at the top of your game—when you are in the zone—are the attributes of a stress-free or dynamically peaceful attitude. Mystic Cool is the zone. It is a dynamically peaceful attitude elevating the mind to generate optimal brain function and put you at your absolute best. The exercise you just did proves that you are more than capable of attaining it. The next challenge is learning to sustain it. Here, too, awareness does most of the work. Watching, learning, and ultimately understanding the sheer power of attitude to transcend limitation can lead to perhaps the most liberating moment in your life.

THE POWER OF ATTITUDE

Attitude is the translation of thought and belief into matching emotions that shape the world we see. It is everything. Attitude determines who we are, what we do, how we do it, and what we ultimately attract and repulse. In this sense, attitude not only creates our reality, it *is* our reality. Attitude is our basic outlook, posture, and inner stance in relation to the outer world that determines the quality of our experience, whatever the circumstance. The word *circumstance*, when dissected, indicates a condition of standing in the midst of a situation that surrounds us. Attitude determines whether our stance will make us larger or smaller than the situation. It decides whether we will rise or fall. Monks and warriors know that a calm, clear, dynamically peaceful attitude makes us larger than circumstances. They also know that a fearful attitude places us at the mercy of what happens. This is what Karl Menninger meant when he said "attitude is more important than facts." Attitude is more important than the past, our education, our social standing, or even money. It is stronger than the world. It immunizes us from stress or causes it. It secures the mind–body connection for optimal health or for disease. It generates the brain chemistry that wires us for success or failure. Attitude is strength, intelligence, and performance. It is the defining inner quality that elevates talent to greatness. It makes a person, a company, a team, a community, or a home. It is the one possession that the world cannot rob from a functional mind, although its sovereignty can be abdicated. For me, no one personifies the power of attitude in sports more than Joe Montana and no one more in life than Viktor Frankl.

Joe Montana

In the 1980s, I had the good fortune of working on the San Francisco 49ers' press team on game day whenever the team played at home. My job was to go into the locker rooms at the end of the game, way down in the bowels of Candlestick Park, and get quotes from the opposing team for the sportswriters. One man I interviewed was Hall of Fame defensive lineman Jack Youngblood, of the Rams. The Rams had just lost a close game, 19–16, primarily due to the near perfect performance of quarterback Joe Montana. I was late getting to the Rams' locker room that day, and the suffocating swarm of reporters circling players and coaches had already formed. This meant I would have to stand at the back of the crowd and catch whatever I could hear over the din of questions. Then I noticed Jack Youngblood, sitting alone on a stool in a far corner of the locker room, pulling adhesive tape off his wrists, so I went over to interview him.

The game was critical to the Rams' playoff hopes, so I asked Youngblood, "What happened to the Rams today?"

"Joe Montana is what happened," Youngblood said with a mix of respect and chagrin in his voice.

"Why weren't you able to stop him?" I asked.

"Because he's the best there is, that's why."

"What makes him the best?"

"His attitude," Youngblood responded. "He believes he can get it done. There are quarterbacks with greater physical tools. Montana doesn't have all that great of an arm and he has sticks for legs, but mentally he's Hercules. His mental game is how he beats you."

"What do mean by mental game?" I asked.

"Like I said, attitude. All things being equal, performance is 100 percent attitude."

I think what Youngblood was saying is that a great athlete takes talent, builds it into skill, and from then on, performance is all about attitude. Attitude takes us beyond our talent. Winners know that the slogan Attitude is Everything is based in fact, not mere idealism, and Montana was a winner. The tougher the situation, the better he became mentally. He responded to the challenge; adversity lifted his performance.

"We threw at Montana a thousand pounds of the meanest, biggest, quickest athletes in the league," Youngblood said. "Each of us hell-bent on crushing him to the ground, and we couldn't force him into a mistake. You just can't stress out Joe Montana, not like some quarterbacks. When the chips are down, I can see the fear in the eyes of some of these other quarterbacks. When you see that, you know you can force them into making errors. Not Joe; he stays cool and calm, and focuses on winning. He didn't get his nickname, Joe Cool, for nothing."

Sports writer Larry Schwartz wrote of Montana, "He possessed an almost mystical calmness in the midst of chaos, especially with the game on the line in the fourth quarter. While others saw turmoil and danger after the snap, Montana saw order and opportunity."[1] All-pro linebacker Mike Singletary said, "You could knock the living snot out of [Montana]. He would get up, spit out the blood and wink at you, and say that was a great hit."[2] That's Mystic Cool.

There is a famous story of Montana in Super Bowl XXIII. There was only 3:10 left in the game. The 49ers had the ball, but they were losing 16–13 and were ninety-two yards away from the end zone. The offense was huddled up, and everyone was tense as the TV network took a commercial break. Montana, in his cool demeanor, turned to lineman Harris Barton and, pointing to the end zone, said, "Isn't that John Candy?"

"What?" replied a perplexed Harris Barton.

"There, in the stands," Montana insisted, "standing near the exit ramp." Some of the players in the huddle turned and looked. Sure enough, it was John Candy. The players laughed, and it broke the tension. Montana then marched the team ninety-two yards, throwing the winning touchdown with thirty-four seconds left.

Years later, I came across a quote of Jack Youngblood that summed up the power of attitude he had emphasized during our interview. "Obstacles don't matter very much," he stated. "Pain or other circumstances can be there, but if you want to do a job bad enough, you'll find a way to get it done."

Viktor Frankl

Mystic Cool is not limited to athletes. Viktor Frankl clearly possessed this quality. Frankl was trained as a physician, specialized in psychiatry, and, later in life, founded existential psychology. He was also a Jew imprisoned by the Nazis at Auschwitz and then Türkheim. In the camps, he provided general medical care to prisoners whenever he could and set up a suicide watch unit. From the hundreds of patients he treated, he found one consistent factor that determined who would survive the extreme mental and physical abuse in the camps; it was attitude. He wrote:

> What was really needed was a fundamental change in our attitude toward life. We had to learn ourselves and, furthermore, we had to teach the despairing men, that it did not really matter what we expected from life, but rather what life expected from us. We needed to stop asking about the meaning of life, and

instead to think of ourselves as those who were being questioned by life—daily and hourly.[3]

Most of the prisoners believed their lives were over, yet in reality, there was an opportunity and a challenge in the experience. "One could make a victory of those experiences," Frankl asserted, "turning life into an inner triumph."[4] Incredibly, in spite of the abject physical and mental deprivation and cruelty, Frankl found that it was possible for one's spiritual life to deepen:

We who lived in the concentration camps can remember the men who walk through the huts comforting others, giving away their last piece of bread. [It offers] sufficient proof that everything can be taken from a man but one thing: the last of the human freedoms—to choose one's attitude in any given set of circumstances, to choose one's own way.[5]

He gives a compelling account of the power of attitude to find beauty, even in the midst of slavery:

As the inner life of the prisoner tended to become more intense, he also experienced the beauty of art and nature as never before. Under their influence, he sometimes even forgot his own frightful circumstances. If someone had seen our faces on the journey from Auschwitz to a Bavarian camp as we beheld the mountains of Salzburg, with their summits glowing in the sunset, through the little barred windows of the prison carriage, he would never have believed that those were the faces of men who had given up all hope of life and liberty.[6]

Growing up, I had a friend who lived on the same street I did in a lower-middle-class neighborhood that had more than its share of bullies. My friend's parents, I learned years later, were Holocaust survivors. I knew by their thick German accent that they were foreigners, but I had no clue as to the horror they had experienced and survived. I was only eight years old and did not know of the Holocaust. All I knew was that their home was the friendliest and safest place on the block. I never left their home without having been made to feel special in some way. This husband and wife came to America with nothing and went on to build a successful retail business. They also put their daughter through law school and their son through medical school.

My family eventually moved and I lost touch with them, but years later, when I was an adult, I bumped into them at a restaurant, and we arranged to get together one Sunday. They told me their story and indulged all the questions my sense of shock had to ask. I came to see that, as humble as this couple was, they were heroic. They may have appeared unremarkable to the average man on the street, but deep down, they possessed extraordinary psychological strength. They possessed the same attitudinal power that makes an athlete great. The Nazis could assail their bodies but not their minds. The guards could strip them of every liberty, but they could not take from them the essential truth of their life, or the love and self-esteem they had known and that still lived in their hearts. A powerful faith, which is perhaps the core of a strong attitude, held their basic human dignity in place. It made an inner victory of outer adversity, even in the midst of brutality.

Viktor Frankl poignantly describes an epiphany of love he experienced in the midst of his brutal existence as he mentally communed with his wife, Tilly.

We were at work in a trench. The dawn was grey around us; grey was the sky above; grey the snow in the pale light of dawn; grey the rags in which my fellow prisoners were clad, and grey their faces. I was again conversing silently with my wife ... struggling to find the reason for my suffering, my slow dying. In a last violent protest against the hopelessness of imminent death, I sensed my spirit piercing through the enveloping gloom. I felt it transcend the hopeless, meaningless world, and from somewhere I heard a victorious, "Yes!" in answer to my question of the existence of an ultimate purpose. At that moment, a light was lit in a distant farmhouse, which stood on the horizon, as if painted there, in the midst of the miserable grey.... For hours I stood hacking at the icy ground. The guard passed by, insulting me, and once again I communed with my beloved. More and more I felt that

she was present, that she was with me; I had the feeling that I was
able to touch her, able to stretch out my hand and grasp hers.... Then,
at that very moment, a bird flew down silently and perched just in
front of me on a heap of soil, which I dug up from the ditch, and
looked steadily at me.[7]

One thought transfixed Frankl during his ordeal: "that love is the ultimate and the highest goal to which man can aspire ... how a man who has nothing left in this world still may know bliss, be it only for a brief moment, in the contemplation of his beloved."[8]

Each of us is capable of attaining this largeness of presence that transcends the circumstances we face, ultimately dignifying the essence of what we are. Frankl admonished those who viewed him and other Holocaust survivors as special people. Rather, he wanted us to understand his life as a demonstration of what is potential in all of us. We are all capable of overcoming stress and the fear beneath it, meeting whatever challenge we face with a dynamically peaceful attitude. Peace is psychological strength. It is the strength that, as David Whyte stated in *Clear Mind, Wild Heart,* "allows us to live in an increasingly difficult world without fear." This does not mean we will never have fears. But it does assert that, like Frankl, we have the capacity for "a largeness of presence that can hold a great deal of losses, difficulties, and possibilities; events that, in the past, we may have not felt large enough to actually confront."[9]

Peace is, by definition, stress free. If peace means anything, it is living a larger life from a deeper vein of being. It means transcending fear through a dynamically peaceful engagement with whatever life presents. This is personal power. As we have seen, these attributes actually produce higher brain function. They tap a deeper intelligence, reaching a more optimal experience of life and actualizing a more productive and constructive mind. Which do you want: a stress-provoking, emotional reaction to a perception of threat, or a dynamically peaceful attitude that makes you larger than circumstances? It is possible to consistently relate to stressors from the quality of mind that is you at the top of your game.

Don Joseph Goewey

PEACE IS WHAT WE WANT

After all is said and done, it is peace most human beings want. We can spend a lifetime looking for peace in all the wrong places. We believe, *If this happens, I'll be at peace.* But the situation rarely delivers or, if it does, it is fleeting. Eventually we learn that peace is not out there. It emanates from inside, as an experience we give ourselves by choosing it. Choosing involves meeting its conditions, most of which are stated below in the Attributes of a Dynamically Peaceful Attitude. The more we meet these conditions, the more our experience of peace deepens. The more it deepens, the more we come to realize that peace is the very heart of what we want. Gathered from various spiritual traditions, each attribute reflects a simple, practical, and yet powerful inner stance we can take in facing the vagaries of life.

ATTRIBUTES OF A DYNAMICALLY PEACEFUL ATTITUDE

A calm, clear sense of personal power and the integrity to assert power without overpowering others

Unafraid

Unhurried

Free of worry

Self-confident

Open-minded, receptive, and accepting

A curiosity that is fully present

Energetic

Resilient

Faith in the face of adversity

Trust in the process

Joy in the challenge

A kind and empathic heart

A willingness to forgive

A disinterest in judging or condemning

A felt connection with one's own heart, with others, and with life itself

An enduring sense of the whole that transcends the fragments

A sense of the sacred

It is clear that these attributes, when viewed as a whole, represent a powerful attitude toward oneself, others, and the world in general. To live in this way is to live the good life. It is an immunity to stress and stressful people, the cure to negative self-talk, and the path to a deeper sense of connection. It is a quality of presence that is alive and engaged. It is a fearless self-confidence that nothing can unsettle.

BRINGING IT HOME

Take a moment to read each attribute and quietly consider what it means to you. Then circle those attributes that correspond with the inner experiences you wrote down at the beginning of this chapter. This should prove to you, if you need proof, that you understand the basic conditions that make life intrinsically rewarding as well as successful. You have proof that you are capable of sustaining a higher experience and translating it into higher achievement.

For those of us who want more of this, the question becomes: how do we do it? We can start by checking those attributes on the above list that could use more of our focus, care, and attention. We can start with just one attribute and commit to bringing it forward, increasingly, into our daily life. Sometimes, applying just one of these attributes fully is all that's needed to realize the full measure of peace in our heart.

Recently, my friend Martha was asked by her mother-in-law to drive a neighbor to a doctor's appointment. "She is very elderly," her mother-in-law said. Martha was surprised to find that the woman was not as elderly as she expected. She looked to be in her mid- to late seventies.

"Do you mind me asking how old you are?" Martha asked on the drive to the doctor.

"Ninety-three," the woman answered.

Martha was astonished. "You look so much younger," she said. "What's your secret?"

"Twenty-three years ago," she answered, "I made the decision to stop worrying. I have not wasted a moment on worry since."

8

The Neuroplasticity of Practice

Heaven never helps the man who will not act.

Sophocles

How do we ground our lives in peace and still improve our situation in a chaotic world? How do we locate the eye of the storm and remain there? How do we make a dynamically peaceful attitude into the force that gently attends to all the plates we are spinning? How do we dissolve the negative thoughts and destructive emotions that pull us back into the storm?

The answer is *practice*. Practice is taking the right step repeatedly until the right step takes us effortlessly, almost automatically, in the direction we want to go. We now understand that we must practice peace, if what we intend is the optimal life experience that a healthy brain naturally generates. We practice an attitude of peace until our experience becomes dynamically peaceful. Neurologically we practice peace until our brain wires for it, infusing peace into every step we take. We know now that this change represents the realization of a powerful brain generating a powerful life that is capable of meaningful action. Studies show that what we want most is a meaningful life that makes a difference. As Irish poet William Yeats illuminated, the greatest difference we make is through our own inner peace.

We can make our minds so like still water that beings
gather around us that they may see ... their own image,
and so live for a moment with a clearer, perhaps even
a fiercer life because of our quiet.

W. B. Yeats

Anyone in their right mind wants a life of peace, and the joy and connection that comes from it. No one in his right mind wants a life of stress. Practice is the discipline that shifts the outcome of what we don't want to the outcome of what we do want.

Oh no, not discipline, some of us cry. *Discipline* can be a loaded word. It can make a thing sound hard. It can also connote punishment, strict behavior, self-denial, or all three at once. Who wants that? In attaining peace, discipline is simple. Discipline is remembering what it is that we want and then choosing it consistently. It gets easier and easier to remember, and easier and easier to choose, simply because we cherish when we have a genuine experience of peace. How could we not? The shift from stress to peace is the difference between feeling poorly and feeling healthy. It is the transition from confused, lackluster, and disconnected to clear, bright, and resonant. It is the transformation of besieged into flourishing. What could be more deserving of our effort and our full intent?

This raises a fundamental question for us to consider: do we truly want peace, enough to meet its conditions? By now, we should understand its worth to us, neurologically, physically, cognitively, emotionally, and spiritually. What could we possibly want that peace cannot bring? Do we want the delight of using our talent, skill, and intelligence to the fullest in achieving what is meaningful to us? Do we want a deep sense of enjoyment that transforms work into a labor of love? Peace offers it. Do we want a quietness that cannot be threatened, a self-confidence that cannot be unsettled, and a vitality that does not fail? Do we want the capacity to meet daily demands with energy and enthusiasm, and to return home at day's end, able to be the person we long to be with our loved ones? Peace bestows it. Do we want to inspire and be inspired, to be empathic and compassionate, and feel a deep, abiding connection with others and with life itself? Peace gives it. Do we want to live a long and healthy life? Peace offers this as well. Seek peace and, in the words of Jesus, "all these things shall be given to you." What more is there to want?

"Human life by its very nature," stated José Ortega y Gasset, "has to be dedicated to something."[1] What offers more than dedicating our life to being at peace? Yet we go looking for peace in all the wrong places. At workshops, I used to conduct a short exercise called "Making a Wish."[2] This segment was intentionally positioned immediately after presenting three studies that showed a weak relationship between finances and satisfaction with life. Billionaires, for example, are only infinitesimally happier than those with average incomes. The Irish, who were comparatively poor at the time of the study, tested as happier than the much wealthier Japanese. In America, where income had doubled in constant dollars between 1960 and 1990, the percentage reporting that they were happy remained steady at 30 percent.[3] During the exercise, people were asked to imagine that they had found the magic lantern, released the genie, and now possessed three wishes that were sure to come true. Despite the prelude to its power, it was rare that anyone wished for lasting inner peace. Overwhelmingly, people wished for things. Money always topped the list. When our sights are primarily on the pot of gold at the end of the rainbow, we miss the rainbow. Often those who chase material wealth much of their lives come to a moment of recognizing that something vital is missing. What we have missed is the experience of peace, and the joy and connection it bestows.

In the opening chapter I related how often I hear clients say that they cannot remember the last time they felt at peace. Some even wonder if peace is attainable this side of paradise, and some wonder if it even exists. Everyone can validate the existence of fear and stress. They can immediately recall the fear of failure but not a time when they were immersed in the sweetness of their own peaceful heart. Equally, they do not think that job performance, health, success, meaningful relationships, or the pursuit of excellence rely on a peaceful attitude. Some even think a peaceful attitude is losing one's edge. Having come this far in the book, you now know that peace takes us to the edge of possibility, in part by healing our *edginess*.

Peace is in all of us. It is networked into our brain; we are born with it. The great mystics tell us that peace defines our very nature. It is on our face when we die, even if we die in battle. As we experienced in the last chapter, attributes of peace emerge in us all the time. The world can assault our peace of mind, but the world cannot destroy it. The study on the Tibetan monks demonstrates that a deeply peaceful relationship with life can actually make us immune to the world's assaults. Peace is always resident in us, in every situation, and at every stage of life. All we need to do is choose it. And the more we choose it, the more we will value it for the worth it adds to our life. If we choose fear this moment, we can choose again; our peaceful nature does not expect us to be perfect. It is always ready whenever we are.

Until we make our intention for peace unequivocal and primary, we will tend to suffer. The more we practice a mindful approach to life— engaging difficult situations peacefully, rather than mindlessly reacting—the more our brain organizes to sustain a more skillful, more enlightened way of being and behaving. As Dr. Daniel Siegel described in his book *The Mindful Brain*, "experience means neural firing."[4] With neural firing can come the "potential to stimulate the growth of new neurons creating new neural networks" to sustain the new experience. This means that, with consistency, the change becomes easier to accomplish; it gradually becomes second nature.

Mercifully, it is never too late; change is possible at any point along the life span. Siegel cites the case study of an elderly client who made significant progress in a short period of time.

I am working with a gentleman who is eighty-seven years old, who came in with a certain kind of personality that was quite restrictive, and he has clearly demonstrated the capacity to massively change his personality style in a very short amount of time. It was his first time in therapy, and he worked [with me] for five months. His wife said she thinks he has had a brain transplant. [This gentleman] said to me, 'It's taken five months to get here. Why did it take so long?' I informed him that it usually takes more than five months to change all these hostile voices in your head, to change the critical attitude towards yourself. I asked him how he did it so quickly. He said, 'You know, I don't have that much time left. I think I had a high motivation.'[5]

A high motivation generates neurological results. His wife may be correct; her husband just may have had something of a brain transplant. It is arguable that neural connections in the brain of Siegel's client changed in response to his changing attitude over the course of therapy. The adage that you can't teach an old dog new tricks does not apply to the brain. The brain is quick to organize around changes we want to effect, when we practice the change with consistency. And it makes changes quickly. It takes the brain just ten days of constraint-induced therapy to rebuild the motor cortex in stroke victims and restore significant use of an arm that physicians once thought was irrevocably damaged.[6] As you recall from chapter 5, it only required:

One week of mentally practicing a five-finger piano exercise for the motor cortex to expand in support of the new skill

Ten weeks for mindfulness therapy to change the brain in obsessive compulsive disorder (Schwartz, 1995)

Eight weeks of cognitive therapy to change the brain in depression (Segal, Mayberg, 2002)

Eight weeks of mindfulness-based stress reduction to shift the prefrontal cortical activity from right to left (negative emotion to positive emotion) in highly stressed workers in a biotech firm (Davidson, Kabat-Zinn, 2003)

Most of the above are extreme situations. Some of these problems, such as stroke damage and obsessive-compulsive disorder, were once considered incurable. Yet the power of neuroplasticity generated significant change in these cases and in a relatively short period of time.

If neuroplasticity is this effective in extreme situations, how much more can it do to transform a brain wired for stress?

It all comes back to practice. Through practice, we are building the brain structure to change stress to ease, fear to peace, powerless to powerful. Through practice, we construct a new autopilot that is wired for a higher, more humane, more fiercely alive intelligence.

The next four chapters in the book outline a practice that meets the conditions for peace.

9

The First Quality of Mystic Cool: Quietly Engaged, Fully Present

It is not in the words. It is not subject to will. It is birds singing,
air moving gently, story coming and going, breath flowing,
back aching, heart beating, sun shining, beholding it all in silence
with an open heart that does not go anywhere.

Toni Packer

The first quality of Mystic Cool is attention. It is the capacity to engage quietly with whatever we are facing and to be fully present in the moment. It is what Eckhart Tolle defined as "the quiet sense of our own presence, our own aliveness that flows into whatever we happen to be doing."[1] Quietly engaged, fully present means we are focused in a way that is spacious. Our openness gives us greater access to information, and our patience with the process enables us to sense the larger relationship emerging from details and to intuit the direction in which things are moving. The obstacle that thwarts this quality of attention is all the racket a mind under stress produces. It is an incessantly thinking, judgmental mind, distracted from the present by pointless preoccupations with the baggage of the past and worries about the future. Shifting these mind-made distortions involves returning our attention to the present moment, quieting the mind, and fearlessly engaging whatever we face.

For most of us, a quiet, fully present moment tends to happen by accident more than by intention. Something external stills the mind—a sunset, the sound of rain beating on the roof, a deer grazing in a meadow, the motion of the sea, and even something as simple as wind chimes. These are dynamically peaceful encounters that have the power to create an unexpected epiphany. However, our more common mode of thinking is rather incessant.

THE FIRST OBSTACLE: INCESSANT THINKING

Incessant thinking can generate all sorts of stressful events, purely in our heads, exciting disturbing emotions that activate a stress reaction, all without anything concrete having actually happened. Our mind can become a nonstop voice, commenting on everything. It has a penchant for taking sides and, at times, is known to reverse its position for no apparent reason. It often points a finger at someone and, in the next breath, turns the same criticism on us. It has been estimated that the average person thinks sixty thousand thoughts a day, 90 percent of which are repetitive. "You are never alone," wrote Byron Katie. "Wherever you are, whomever you're with, the voice in your head goes with you, whispering, nagging, enticing, judging, shaming, guilt tripping, or even yelling at you."[2]

The "thinking" mind takes for granted that it is who we are, and we tend to go along. In the mental confusion it generates, we find it next to impossible to locate a meaningful sense of self. The thinking mind thinks: *I am you, and your life is this story I am telling you and constantly revising.* It is the mind-made, brain-made story that Shakespeare called a tale told by an idiot, full of sound and fury, and signifying nothing.

Few forms of expression can become as histrionic as incessant thinking. Below is an example. As you read it, infuse it with the same exaggerated emotion you might experience on a tense ride to work with your brain racing from a venti-size cup of Starbucks coffee.

POINTLESSLY PREOCCUPIED

@#$%^&*()_+!!! Got a meeting with George at ten, and the stuff at the cleaners, can't forget that even though I don't want to go to that party, why is she making me go? I just want to come home and put my feet up. I need to prepare for George, I don't get his agenda, and what about that tie he wore last week? Is he color-blind? Oh, got to call Linda about lunch, she'll probably make me pay again, she just sits there when the check comes, I hate that. So what do I need to do to prepare for George? I should finish that report, and the brown shoes with the black suit, does he even look in the mirror in the morning? He needs to lose weight. Oh no, I didn't bring my gym bag, not again, oh there it is, thank god, I got to go today, I'm putting on weight, it's so hopeless, weight off weight right back on, NO CARBS TODAY AND NO SUGAR EITHER!!! @#$%^&*()_+@#$%^&*()_+@#$%^&*()+@#$%^&*()+@#$%^&*()+@#$%^&*()

○　○　○

This stream of consciousness is really a stream of *un*consciousness that never seems to stop. The pointlessly preoccupied narrative you just read could go on for three more pages and not capture the incessant thinking that can happen on the walk from the parking lot to our office. We think so incessantly that the notion that we could turn it off and be still seems impossible. Sometimes, usually late at night, we can paint ourselves into a tight corner with a stream of fearful thinking. If, by some act of grace, we are able to escape it, we realize, looking back from a safer shore, that much of what we thought was delusional. It was largely painful thoughts generating fearful images that batter us into feeling separate and alone in a hostile world. "[Incessant thinking] comes between you and yourself," wrote Eckhart Tolle, "between you and your fellow man and woman, between you and nature, between you and God."[3]

We cannot escape this form of mind by trying to figure it out. We cannot change it or will it away. We can, however, transcend it. "When thoughts are whirling about," wrote meditation teacher Toni Packer, "we can let them be like dancing snowflakes in empty space."[4] If we could acquire a little more space between thoughts, meaning a little more peace and quiet between the fears that haunt us, it is inevitable that we will feel increasingly safer, happier, and neurologically, gain more and more access to the enormous power of our brain. Who, in their right mind, would not volunteer for that?

Watching the Thinker[5]

We are going to practice watching the thinker to see if there is an exit we can find that leads away from all the noise into a quiet, open space. The Sufi poet Rumi wrote: "Out beyond ideas of right-doing and wrong-doing, there is a field. I'll meet you there." The purpose of this exercise is to take us out beyond the chatter in our mind to see if there actually is a quieter, saner field of experience inside of us.

1. Sit or lie comfortably. Close your eyes. All you are asked to do is observe. Simply be with whatever your mind generates. Notice what you are thinking, feeling, and perceiving. Don't become involved in the thoughts. Don't judge them or try to change them. Simply observe.

2. If your mind gets lost in a proliferation of thought or makes judgments and evaluations, observe this. Notice the thoughts that come and go, the residue of emotion they carry, and the pictures they paint. Stand back from it and simply notice. At first, it may seem there is nothing but chatter and chaos. Do not judge or condemn what you hear.

3. The mind will present you with the impulse to do something other than this process. Ignore that impulse and bring your attention to the breath.

4. The body will demand attention. Ignore this as well, returning attention to the breath.

5. After a few minutes of consciously observing, you will begin to sense the aspect of mind that is doing the observing. You will begin to reach beyond the chatter, simply by witnessing it.

6. Soon you realize: *There is a voice chattering away, and I am simply observing it, neutrally.* "This *I am* realization," stated Eckhart

Tolle, "this sense of your own presence, is not a thought. It arises from beyond the mind."[6]

7. Recall Rumi's words once again: "Out beyond ideas of right-doing and wrong-doing, there is a field. I'll meet you there."

8. Meet yourself in Rumi's field. Relax into the unencumbered space of being. Allow it to expand with each breath. It is the gateway to a quiet mind, setting you free to simply be.

Starting the Day

Starting the morning with the Watching the Thinker process can change the quality of your day. All that is required is fifteen minutes. It is, in part, a classroom for bringing our stress pattern into greater awareness. It offers a kind of laboratory for observing the reactive thoughts, feelings, and perceptions that generate stress. We see first-hand how easily these proliferate when we attach to them, and how, just as easily, they pass into oblivion when we detach nonjudgmentally, by returning our attention to the breath. Through the process we begin to understand with greater clarity that emotions are not facts, thoughts are not truth, perception is not reality, and none of it is essentially you. Thich Nhat Hahn, the Vietnamese monk whom Martin Luther King Jr. nominated for the Nobel Peace Prize, recommends adding gratitude to the process. "Every morning, when we wake up," he wrote, "we have twenty-four brand new hours to live. What a precious gift! We have the capacity to live in a way that these twenty-four hours will bring peace, joy, and happiness to ourselves and others."[7]

A Shortcut: The Clear Button[8]

As we have seen, most stress reactions begin with fearful thinking. When we collapse the thought pattern, before it proliferates into negative emotions and perceptions of threat, we can thwart a stress reaction. Normally, at work it is not possible to take a fifteen-minute break to quiet the mind. But here is a shortcut we can use. It is called "The Clear Button."

Imagine for a moment that you are speaking with someone and the discussion is beginning to cause you some anxiety. You are worried that a decision is taking shape that you do not favor. You begin to feel edgy, and a pattern of defensive thinking starts to surface. Losing your composure is the last thing you want. The Clear Button is a tool that can collapse the escalating pattern of stress.

1. Become aware of the stress you are feeling.

2. Notice the thinking process that is driving the stress you experience.

3. Imagine a button on your chest or palm that ends thinking.

4. This kinetic property is important, so locate the imagined button on your body.

5. Take three easy breaths, counting them out. Imagine a different color for each number.

6. Now press your button and imagine that your mind clears completely.

7. Focus attention on the next two breaths and relax as you softly exhale.

8. Bring your awareness into the present moment and quietly notice the quality of aliveness restored in you.

9. With this simple ten-second exercise, you have busted incessant thinking and the stress it was about to escalate.

10. Re-engage with the situation and consciously choose to be at peace, regardless of circumstances or outcome, confident in the clarity your calm now affords you.

THE SECOND OBSTACLE: THE JUDGING MIND

The judging mind is the second obstacle to quieting our thoughts and orienting ourselves to the present moment. As we have seen, Mars, or the emotional brain, is constantly assessing the environment, jumping to conclusions when it finds in memory even the slightest match between the current situation and a past trauma. The same emotional memory that nature evolved in animals to catalog dangerous smells, sounds, tastes, and movements has morphed in human beings to form all of our likes and dislikes, our tastes and distastes—from people to clothes to food to mates. We have taken it a step further to form opinions, prejudices, and judgments about people and situations. At times, these judgments do not have a kind thing to say about anyone, including us. This judgmental mind compares, labels, criticizes, stereotypes, and distorts, often believing everything it thinks is true, simply because it thinks it.

We Are Never Upset for the Reason We Think

Once at lunch, a friend of mine caught himself disliking a man to whom he had just been introduced. It was completely irrational. My friend did not know the man from Adam. There was no history on which to base his dislike. The man was polite and friendly, and yet my friend did not like him. It wasn't until the lunch was nearly over that it dawned on him. This man bore a likeness to a man who had caused him pain when he was younger. That was the impetus. His emotional brain had zeroed in, scanned its memory banks, and found a face that matched the man who had betrayed him. Instantly, the old feelings of pain, distrust, and dislike were evoked, placing my friend on guard. It is the way emotional memory works. Later, my friend realized the game his mind was playing. Had he not, it is likely he would have said something disparaging about this person when his back was turned. How many people we have cold-shouldered or belittled as a result of the emotional brain interpreting the present as the past? In truth, we are seeing something that is not there—something that is not true in the present moment—although at the time, we believe it is. Our emotional brain is reacting to the painful past, disturbing our sense of security, and it is prone to attack in some way when insecure.

Negative Self-Talk

Often, the person with whom we feel the most insecure, and therefore tend to judge most harshly, is ourselves. These judgments and attacks take the form of a negative inner dialogue called negative self-talk. It is perhaps the single most stress-provoking phenomenon in our lives. It can literally send the body into an uproar. Most of the negativity stems from parents who harped on what they perceived as our faults, coaches and teachers who criticized our efforts, or jealous siblings who ridiculed us to feel better about themselves. When these judgments harden into beliefs, making them seem true, we become part of what the emotional brain dislikes, meaning we do not like ourselves.

Psychological Projection

Most of what I have just described happens below conscious awareness. When the burden of our negative self-image is more than we can bear, we project it onto other people in the form of judgments. For example, a few years ago I had been eating poorly and had put on weight, nearly ten pounds. It bothered me, but I just could not discipline my eating habits. One day an old acquaintance visited me at work. I had not seen her in a couple years. She was an attractive woman but had gained an excessive amount of weight since I'd last seen her. It bothered me, but I didn't mention it. We talked pleasantly for a while, and then I walked her to the front door and hugged her goodbye. As I walked back to my office, I was judging her. *She looks awful*, I thought. *What's the matter with her? Why doesn't she do something about her weight?* My mood was actually turning to disgust for a person I valued. On the way back to my office, I stopped off at the bathroom. As I passed the large mirror over the sink, I caught a glimpse of my pudgy form and muttered under my breath, *I hate you*.

I had probably been saying that to myself for years, but that day I heard myself and it shocked me. Out of the blue, I remembered my uncle, who had been dead for some time. My uncle never made much of himself, and was a source of embarrassment to my mother and grandmother. As a result, whenever I came home with a poor grade or when I was lazy, my parents would admonish me with: "You are going to turn out just like your Uncle Tommie." Later in life, my uncle became obese. After that, whenever I put on weight, I worried I would end up like him.

As I stood there in front of the bathroom mirror, I suddenly understood it all. It was not fat I wanted to lose. It was the weight of failing at life, represented by my Uncle Tommie and, by extension, anyone else who was overweight. I could see that my disgust with my friend represented not only the fear but the belief that I would fail. It was a lesson that, whenever I judge, the water runs deeper than I think. When we are judging another person, we are often projecting our own negative belief about ourselves, ingrained in us by social conditioning.

IDENTIFYING THE CRITICAL VOICE

Martin Seligman of University of Pennsylvania, one of the founders of positive psychology, has developed a proven way of quieting these critical voices in our head. The first step is awareness. It is recognizing the negative self-talk triggered when we make a mistake or encounter difficulty.

The Critical Voice Inquiry[9]

The following process engages a mindful inquiry into negative self-talk in order to refute it.

1. Think of the last time you made a mistake, felt embarrassed by a behavior or action, or were challenged by bad news for which you felt somehow responsible. See yourself in the place where it happened. What time of day was it? Imagine yourself transported to that moment.

2. If it involved another person, see their face, hear their voice.

3. What did you feel? Depressed, angry, shocked, defeated, stressed?

4. During or afterward, what critical, negative statements did you say to yourself?

5. Make the experience of it real. Make it vivid. Make it now.

6. When you are ready, take out a piece of paper.

7. Write at the top *The Mistake* or *The Adversity*. Then briefly describe the situation.

8. Next write the heading *The Critical Voice Said*. Then write down what your critical voice said. Example: *I hate myself. You fool. You idiot. How could you have done that? How stupid!*

9. Under this, write the heading *The Belief Behind the Criticism*. Then identify the belief that underlies the criticism. Example: *I am irresponsible. I am stupid. I won't get this right. I am worthless. I can't be trusted.*

10. Last, write the heading *What Does this Mean for the Future?* Write what consequences your critical voice forecasts for the future.

Refuting the Critical Voice

Now let's see if we can transcend the judging, critical mind to achieve a more optimistic self-view. We are going to challenge the critical voice.

1. What is the critical voice saying that is distorted or factually incorrect? Ask: is this critical statement about me, my character, and my ability true all the time and in all situations? Of course this is not true. So let it go by not believing it.

2. Identify what you did that was positive. Example: *I made mistakes, but I also succeeded in another way, or I succeeded in this situation at another time.* Document it for yourself in writing. Become your own character witness.

3. Scan for contributing factors that caused the mistake or problem. Negative self-talk puts all the blame on you. Look at the situation as a good friend would.

4. If there is some factual truth in what the critical voice states, acknowledge it. It may be a weakness you need to manage better

or a blind spot you need help to see. Acknowledge it in an undefended fashion, without judging or condemning yourself. None of us are perfect.

5. Negative self-talk is often fixed on worst case scenarios, exaggerating outcomes and consequences. Ask: how likely are these dire consequences?

6. Next, recall your initial intention in this situation. Make it count. If your hopes were realized, what would the outcome be? Set this against the condemnation and bleak forecast of the critical voice. Both are mind-made. Which infuses your sense of personal power with enthusiasm, hope, and optimism? Choose between the two. The choice should be obvious.

7. Look back on this situation. Think of one positive, true quality you see in yourself that can turn the situation in a positive direction. Open yourself to this thought until it lights up with feeling. Then dedicate the rest of the day to experiencing this feeling.

Seligman stated, "Learned optimism works not through an unjustifiable positivity about the world but through the power of 'non-negative thinking.'"[10] Joel Osteen, author of *Become a Better You*, counseled, "Use your words to bless your life."[11] Strong thoughts and beliefs exist as complex neurological pathways. The more we break negative thought patterns by no longer believing them, the easier it becomes to invoke the positive. It represents an increase in neural firing, called kindling. Kindling gradually replaces negative self-talk with self-esteem.

Today, as you go out into your world, commit to judging less. Hold the intention to judge nothing that occurs today. You will find that during the day your energy will be much higher. Judging ourselves and others is stressful, and stress depletes energy.

10

The Second Quality of Mystic Cool: Calm and Clear Inside, Regardless of Outside

*The last of the human freedoms—to choose one's attitude
in any given set of circumstances, to choose one's own way.*

Viktor Frankl

The second quality of Mystic Cool is internal calm and clarity, regardless of what is happening externally. It is an attitude of calm tapping our wisdom to determine the right thing to do. In this way, our calm renders us larger than circumstances. The summit we can attain through this attitude is a fearless self-confidence that problems cannot unsettle. It is analogous to the calm-under-siege that is core to military training. It is the threshold of the fortitude that Dr. Al Siebert, author of *The Resiliency Advantage*, has identified in studies on the inner nature of highly resilient survivors.

Siebert has studied people who have survived some of the most difficult situations imaginable, from shark attacks to avalanches to war.[1] He found that an attitude of calm is the chief factor in determining who survives a life-threatening crisis. A calming attitude allows us to pay close attention to what is happening, to assess what needs to be done, and to act decisively when the time comes. About 10 percent of the population possesses this trait. However, Siebert asserts that it is a trait anyone can learn, though few have bothered to do so. We can learn to develop this trait in the boot camp of everyday life. We can cultivate this quality in the way we work through the everyday pressures of traffic jams, deadlines, difficult people, financial problems, strategic breakdowns, and the like.

The obstacles to calm and clarity are generally emotional, typically when we feel out of control or overwhelmed. We transcend a loss of control through the recognition that, while we may have influence, the only real control we have in most situations is our attitude. Attitude is sufficient to regain control over our inner experience, regardless of what is happening outside. We transcend overwhelm when we maintain a clear inner purpose as we attempt to achieve the external goals aimed at improving our situation.

The First Obstacle: The Loss of Control

Obviously, loss of control in important situations can make us anxious or depressed. There is much in life over which we have no control. Loss of control, as an emotional reaction, is often rooted in the lack of clarity about what we do and do not control, captured poignantly in Reinhold Niebuhr's serenity prayer:

> *God, grant me the serenity to accept the things I cannot change, the courage to change the things I can, and the wisdom to know the difference.*

The belief that we control events can actually increase the odds of failing. In a study of the illusion of control in a population of traders working in investment banking, researchers found that traders who believed they had more control than was true—the term for it is *high illusion of control*—performed poorly and earned significantly less money.[2] "The desire to be in control, the illusion of being in control, and the hope of being in control," stated the mystic Gangaji, "are all based on the megalomaniacal belief that we know when and what the outcome should be."[3] We rarely do. Nor do we need to. We can trust an attitude of calm to provide the clarity for what to do and when to do it.

The Control Exercise—Getting Clear

The following exercise can help you clarify the degree of control you realistically have in most situations by deconstructing a recent situation that was particularly stressful. The stressful event you identified in chapter 6 can also be used.

1. Take a moment, bringing this situation to mind. Feel the situation. What was your emotional state? What were you thinking at the time? Make it real by visualizing the time of day, who may have been involved, and any other detail that brings it into focus. If a person was involved, see his or her face.

2. Take out a piece of paper and format it by drawing a line vertically down the full length of the paper, about two inches in from the right. At the top of the right column, write *Rating*.

3. On the left side of your worksheet, delineate those key elements present in the situation that can be measured in terms of the amount of control you had over them. For example, Joe attended a meeting held in a noisy restaurant at the airport in order to accommodate his client. The client had just flown in and had only thirty minutes before leaving to catch his connecting flight. The client was fatigued and cranky from his travel. He surprised Joe with requests for significant changes in an agreement Joe thought had been finalized. These descriptions are key elements. Identify up to six of yours.

4. When you have identified your key elements, rate each one for the level of control you perceive you had in the situation. The scale is 0 to 5. Zero signifies no control; 5 signifies complete control; 2–4 are the levels in between. Record the number in your Rating column.

5. When you have completed the form, go over your ratings. See if you have overrated or underrated your assessment of how much real control you had.

The Control Exercise is a process I often conduct in trainings. In spite of the lecture I give on the power of attitude prior to the exercise, few—if any—of the participants list their attitude as a key element under their control in the situation. Yet in many of life's situations, our attitude is the only real control we have. It is the only element that realistically merits a 5. Often we are overly focused on what others will or won't do, what we will or won't get, or we're caught in conflict with elements of the circumstance that we do not like. The power of attitude flies right out the window.

Look back over the worksheet. Can you see how little control you have over the vagaries of life? Can you see, had you asserted the power of a positive attitude, how your experience might have been different? Can you see how your attitude might have had impact?

Regaining Control[4]

When conflict raises its ugly head, we can regain self-control by exercising the power of choice. The following process can help to reorient the mind by exposing the problem to what Eckhart Tolle called "the only sane choices in any conflict."[5] Again, bring to mind the stressful situation you just processed. Read each of the following three decisions in regard to the situation, and see how each feels to you.

Decide to change the situation—this means continuing to work on shifting the situation.

Walk away from the situation—close the chapter on this part of your life, without animosity. Let it go as you would anything that no longer serves you.

Accept the situation completely—let go of any need to change the situation or person. Accept the situation or the person as is.

For the moment, suspend the need to ponder your choice or argue over it. Simply permit yourself to see how each of the three choices feels. Which one resonates with peace? This is your best indicator of which choice to make. Once your feeling is clear, you have the option of following through or not.

THE SECOND OBSTACLE: OVERWHELM

Overwhelm is the next obstacle to the experience of calm and clarity inside. The pursuit of multiple external goals without a clear inner purpose is a prescription for overwhelm. External goals are exclusively focused on improving our situation in the world. These goals are about shaping the world, as much as possible, to meet our needs and preferences. The world, of course, does not readily bend to our desires. We can approach it with diligence, cover all the bases, and jump through its hoops, and still, it breaks our windows, breaks our bones, and breaks our hearts. It is not in the nature of the world to give us peace. It gives us problems and is indifferent to our suffering. Below is the parable of Buddha and the farmer that poignantly illustrates this truth.

The Eighty-Fourth Problem

A well-to-do farmer had heard that the Buddha was a wonderful teacher and went to him, seeking relief from his suffering.

"I'm a landowner," he told the Buddha, "And I love to watch my people working in the fields and to see my crops grow. But last summer we had a drought and nearly starved. This summer, we had too much rain and some of my crops did poorly."

The Buddha sat and listened to the farmer.

"I have a wife too. She's a good woman and a wonderful wife. But sometimes she nags me. To tell the truth, sometimes I grow tired of her."

The Buddha continued to listen as the farmer went on.

"I have three children. They are basically good, and I am very proud of them. But sometimes they don't listen to me or pay me the respect I deserve." The farmer carried on like this at length, listing his woes, and when he was finished, he turned to the Buddha with great anticipation, waiting for him to provide the answer that would solve all his problems.

"I cannot help you," said the Buddha.

"What do you mean you can't help me?" responded the farmer.

"Simply that everyone has problems," the Buddha replied. "In fact, everyone has eighty-three problems. You may solve one now and then, but another is sure to take its place. Everything is subject to change. Life is impermanent. Everything you have built will return to dust; everyone you love is going to die. You, yourself, are going to die someday. Therein dwells the problem of all problems, and there is nothing you can do about it."

The farmer was chagrined. "What kind of teaching is this? How can it possibly help me?"

"Perhaps it will help you with the eighty-fourth problem," answered the Buddha.

"What is the eighty-fourth problem?" asked the farmer anxiously.

"The problem of not wanting any problems," replied the Buddha.[6]

The world can threaten to overwhelm us, but here, too, we have a choice to exercise. We can choose the one thing the world cannot take from us without our permission—our peace of mind. Peace is not of the world; its calm and clarity come from within.

The Nature of External Goals

Eckhart Tolle, in *The Power of Now*, defines some characteristics of external goals. They involve a multitude of steps. A good example is the process of buying a house. Many steps are involved, with scores of papers to read and sign. Next, external goals require decisions, which itself involves finding answers to a wide variety of questions, from mundane to critical, such as: what color, how long, what size, how much, is this really what I want, is there a better way of getting it, can I afford it, is this the right decision? Often our indecision is the result of how overwhelmed we feel with all that our goals entail. It can make the process feel interminable. Last, external goals are largely future-oriented; they represent a plan we are working toward.

Complicating matters is that we usually are pursuing multiple goals at once. They involve every level of life. When I was younger, I believed—

without ever thinking it through—that when I finally learned to handle all the plates I had spinning in the air, I would experience peace. I was never able to keep them all going at once or to reach perfect balance. Every day it seemed one or another of them crashed to the ground and shattered. I finally accepted the fact that the nature of the world is as impersonal as the law of gravity, and just as unyielding. Eventually, I learned that if I wanted peace, I would have to find it within.

An Inner Purpose

There is a solution to the overwhelm that multiple external goals can cause; it is giving primacy to an internal goal of peace. Whereas external goals are intrinsically complicated, inner peace is exquisitely simple.

An internal goal or inner purpose, as Tolle calls it, involves only one step—the step we are taking. It is concerned with the only time there is—this moment right now. And it asks only one question: do we want peace or fear? Centering ourselves in this moment and taking this next step with dignity is the end of overwhelm.

Dr. Gerald Jampolsky, father to a school of psychology based on attitude, goes as far as to say that when clarity becomes the thing we want, peace of mind becomes our only goal. "Purity of heart," stated the great philosopher Søren Kierkegaard, "is to want one thing only."

Flow

An external goal approached with an inner purpose of peace creates the optimal experience of flow. As we approach our goals, the more we make the choice to be at peace, the more we will realize the dynamic experience that inner peace generates. The conscious choice to be at peace means we are quietly engaged and fully present. This quality of presence allows us to see more, engage more, learn more, and be more respectful and ethical in all our dealings. When we are peacefully engaged with work, memory is better, energy is higher, emotions are stable, facts are neutral, and morality guides us. Our attention is fluid.

We can draw back to see the big picture or shift focus to zero-in on a detail.

To be at peace also means we are not afraid of life and its problems. This, in and of itself, makes us larger than circumstances. Letting go of fear naturally empowers peace. Gradually, our peace gives rise to a joyful curiosity that is alive with freedom and possibility. We feel optimistic because we feel in control of our direction. A fearless self-confidence sometimes takes hold. We begin to feel there is nothing we cannot do, no goal we cannot achieve, no obstacle we cannot overcome. It is a joyful feeling. As joy turns into flow, it transforms effort into ease. Work becomes fun. The Buddhists call it effortless effort. It seems all we need to manage is our vigilance for peace; everything else seems to take care of itself. The dots seem to connect themselves. Pieces of the puzzle seem to fall into place. Time, stress, and self-doubt nearly disappear. We are swept along in a vibrant flow of calm, producing optimal brain function that approximates genius. Some even feel that they are being carried along by a force greater than themselves—one that transcends the limitations of physical reality. Artists call it the muse; mystics call it ah-ha. Athletes and business people call it the zone. It is the joy of excelling and begins with the choice to be at peace. It is the joy of being alive as we do whatever we happen to be doing. Being, doing, and living in this way is intrinsically rewarding, and the reward it bestows is far greater than anything an external goal can offer.

We can develop the ability to evoke a dynamically peaceful attitude from day to day, and over the course of a day, as we transition from one project or goal to another. Simply sit calmly for a moment before beginning a task. Feel the power and value of an inwardly peaceful stance. Bring to mind the goal or aim of the work you are about to perform. Feel your enthusiasm, not only for achieving the goal but for the opportunity to excel. Imagine that your resolve is an arrow headed straight for the bull's eye. Then let go of the outcome. Remember the inner experience of flow you want to sustain as you work, and trust the process.

An inner purpose of peace does not mean that likes and dislikes vanish. There are chores we would rather not do, even within projects we enjoy. A peaceful attitude enables us to accept what we must do, instead of struggling, complaining, or procrastinating. We can use the awareness exercise on page 103 to notice when our dislikes raise an irritated voice in protest of a job that needs to be handled. The simple act of awareness can reduce the tension we have tended to experience in having to do what we don't like to do.

Reframing

An effective way to strengthen the inner goal of peace is to visualize, in advance, difficult situations we will be called upon to handle, and frame them in an attitude of peace.

PreAttitude: Visualizing Peace in a Place of Conflict[7]

A tool that can accomplish this reframing is PreAttitude. PreAttitude helps ground our inner purpose by imagining greater self-control. It is an effective way to prepare for any situation we perceive as intense. It can help us approach difficult people and situations that we have not handled well in the past. It is a wonderful way to prepare for coming home from a stressful day.

1. Pick a specific place or time when you felt happy and peaceful. Make it real, vivid. Remain in this peaceful state briefly, until the feeling is clear and strong.

2. Now bring to mind a person or situation you perceive as difficult or stressful, and imagine you are there right now. Make the future become now.

3. Bring the happy, peaceful feeling you have been visualizing into this situation.

4. See yourself confident, optimistic, energetic, and at peace in this situation. Imagine that you do not give away your sense of personal power.

5. Imagine you are open-minded, not so focused on the outcome that it pulls you away from the peace you feel.

6. Imagine that you feel increasingly larger than the situation simply because you are no longer afraid of it or overwhelmed.

7. If other people are involved, imagine you are able to communicate what you want to say and are also able to listen carefully to what they have to say, without antagonism.

8. Imagine that your sense of calm and clarity remains firm, regardless of what anyone does or does not do.

9. At the end of the encounter, see yourself at peace, still feeling confident and energetic, whatever the outcome.

The only place we ever need to find is the quiet center of our own peaceful nature. From there, whatever we extend to the world will be kind, positive, and ultimately successful—which is the next segment of the book.

The last two qualities of Mystic Cool are about extending this dynamically peaceful and positive nature to create meaningful relationships at every level of life.

11

The Third Quality of Mystic Cool: Connected and Connecting

We are neurally constructed to feel connected to each other.

Daniel Siegel, MD

The term *cerebral* or *brainy* is often used to describe a person who is remote, living in his or her own analytical world of thought, emotionally unavailable and socially awkward. These characteristics could not be less related to the neural properties of the brain. The human brain is a social organ, and its neural architecture is built for interpersonal connection.[1] Schizophrenia and autism are disorders that make it difficult, if not impossible, for people to connect and feel connected to others. Both disorders appear to be linked to the impairment of neural architecture.[2] The natural inclination of a functional brain is to connect. Separation makes the brain nervous. Expose an infant primate to an unpleasant stressor, place her in a room with primates that are strangers, and the stress reaction will exacerbate. Place the infant in a room with other primates who are her friends and family, and the stress reaction is mitigated.

Robert Sapolsky of Stanford related a story about a boy from a psychologically abusive setting who was hospitalized with zero growth hormone in his bloodstream.[3] Chronic stress had completely shut down the body's growth system. Over the next two months he developed a close relationship with the nurse at the hospital—undoubtedly the first normal relationship he had ever had—and soon, amazingly enough, his growth hormone levels zoomed back to normal. However, when the nurse went on vacation, the boy's levels dropped again and then returned to normal immediately after her return. "Think about it," Sapolsky commented. "The rate at which this child was depositing calcium in his bones could be explained entirely by how safe and loved he was feeling in the world."

"The experience of separateness arouses anxiety," wrote Erich Fromm, the great social psychologist. "It is, indeed, the source of all anxiety."[4] We are wired to connect with one another. A failure to connect is a failure to thrive. The research on this point is overwhelming. Connection is the single most important factor in determining how long we live. To our brain, love and survival are synonymous, which is why our brain seduces, coaxes, entreats, and drives us to love. The research of Dr. Helen Fisher of Rutgers into the biochemical, neurological, and social foundations of love has led her to conclude that love is not an emotion; it is a drive more powerful than the sex drive, emanating from the engine of the brain.[5]

Two obstacles that block connection are a conditional regard for others and an unwillingness to forgive. A relationship based on conditional regard sustains connection as long as conscious or unconscious expectations are met. When someone does not live up to our expectations, we withdraw our regard, separate ourselves emotionally, and sometimes we even end the relationship. In essence, conditional regard means we cherish what we require another to be or do for us more than we cherish the person. We are focused on getting more than giving. Blame trumps understanding; judgment trumps acceptance. The conflict this generates is played out in divorce courts and lawsuits every day. The fact is, we human beings tend to disappoint others' expectations. We tend to follow our own drum, sometimes passively, sometimes assertively. On top of that, we are prone to make mistakes.

A conditional regard is simply not a practical approach to staying connected with a human being. Marriage counselors know that the primary impetus for change in a relationship is the complete acceptance of one another—as is. It is true in every kind of relationship. Complete acceptance is what makes a relationship safe and ultimately liberating. Its spaciousness can free us to find ourselves.

Few relationships achieve acceptance without first passing through forgiveness. Often, enduring marriage and friendships owe their longevity to a time when one person was willing to forgive the other. An unwillingness to forgive breaks the bond.

THE ROSETO EFFECT

The reward we earn for loving unconditionally is a longer life. The first study to reveal the biological primacy of interpersonal connection was the Roseto Study.[6] It has come to be called the Roseto Effect. Forty years ago, medical researchers were drawn to Roseto, Pennsylvania, by a bewildering statistic that defied medical logic. Rosetans were nearly immune to a stress-related disease that is the number-one cause of death in America—heart disease. Over a seven-year period, no Roseto men under forty-seven had died of a heart attack. For older men, the rate was barely half that of men in neighboring towns.

Even more mystifying was the fact that the residents led hard lives, the kind that would typically lead to an early grave. The people of the village were poor. The men smoked and drank wine liberally. They spent their days doing backbreaking and dangerous jobs in the belly of slate quarries. They ate a Mediterranean diet, but it was not the heart-healthy kind. Their diet was laden with fat. They were poor immigrants and could not afford to import olive oil from their homeland. Instead they fried their sausages and browned their meatballs in lard. The resulting hefty bodies, however, contained unusually healthy hearts. How could it be? The researchers tested and tested and pored over the data, but none of the medical data could explain it. Nor was there a correlation between their healthy hearts and genetics or physiological anomalies.

Perhaps, the researchers thought, the explanation for this phenomenon was social in nature. Perhaps it was in the character of the people, which was unusually vivacious. "The atmosphere of Roseto was gay and friendly," the researchers discovered, "reflecting an enthusiastic and positive attitude toward life." They are simple, warm, and very hospitable." Most striking to the researchers was their genuinely positive regard for one another: "They are mutually trusting and mutually supportive," the report added.[7]

When researchers turned their attention to social factors, they discovered two interesting facts. Both the crime rate and applications for public assistance in the community were nonexistent. When they took a closer look, they found that Rosetans took pride in taking care of their families. Nearly all the homes contained three generations, and elders were revered. Mealtimes were much more than a matter of eating. They were a time for the family to gather and to strengthen intergenerational ties. In warm weather, villagers took evening strolls and stopped in to visit with neighbors. Community events were also common in Roseto. There were many social clubs and church events, in which the whole community took part. At Mary's Luncheonette every customer was known by name and every day children flocked in for an after-school snack. After further study, the researchers concluded the reason for the villagers' good health was the deep sense of connection with family and community.

Although the villagers were poor, they managed to send their children to college at a rate above the national average. By the close of World War II, Roseto had developed a white-collar class and was prospering. They could afford televisions, and the wider world charmed the minds of the young. By the 1970s, the town had suburbanized, diminishing the old neighborhoods; the church was no longer the center of the community, and the nuclear family was the norm. Most of those who went off to college resettled in the big city, where the best jobs were. Others married people from out of town and moved away. Within a decade, the Roseto Effect had dissolved. In 1971, the village recorded its first death of a person under the age of forty-five from coronary disease. The traditional communal experience that enabled people to live longer, healthier lives had eroded. One of the young people who left the village for the big city stated, "I'm sorry [we] moved; everything is modern here and we have everything we need here, except people."[8]

Major studies done at Harvard, Carnegie Mellon, and UCLA have corroborated the Roseto Effect. It is now well established that mutual respect, cooperation, and a sense of belonging contribute significantly to people's health and longevity. Social isolation, a limited self-interest, and lack of concern for others can shorten a lifespan. Stepchildren, for example, have significantly higher levels of stress hormones than children whose parents have remained married to each other. Yet even a defining external factor such as this can be overcome by a deepened sense of connection.

William Kell at Ohio State University studied juvenile delinquents to assess which interventions predicted a troubled adolescent's healthy adjustment at some point in the future. Certainly, genetics and environment predispose a delinquent to less than adequate adjustment. However, the study showed that these were not definitive. What predicted a sustained positive adjustment, in 84 percent of cases, was an increase in self-understanding and self-acceptance facilitated through the empathy of someone who cared.[8] The quality of what happens between us generates something within us that is stronger than what happened in the past.

FRIENDS ARE GOOD MEDICINE

One of the great philosophers of the last century, George Santayana, commented, "One's friends are that part of the human race with which one can be human."[9] The freedom our friends afford us to relax and simply be the human being we are carries significant health benefits. Researchers have found in study after study that people who maintain close friendships reduce the risk of death and disease. The famed Nurses' Health Study from Harvard Medical School, the longest running investigation of factors that influence women's health, found that the more friends women had, the less likely they were to develop physical impairments as they aged. They were more likely to lead a happier life. The results were so significant, the researchers concluded, that not having close friends or confidantes was as detrimental to one's health as smoking or carrying extra weight. When the researchers looked at how well the women functioned after the death of their spouse, they found that even in the face of this loss, women with close friends and confidantes were more likely to survive the experience without any new physical ailments or loss of vitality. Those without friends were not so fortunate.

TEND AND BEFRIEND

A study at UCLA,[10] based on an analysis of hundreds of biological and behavioral studies, found a significant difference between the way men and women respond to stress. "Men often react to stress with a fight-or-flight response," stated principal investigator Shelley E. Taylor, "but women are more likely to manage their stress with a tend-and-befriend response by nurturing their children or seeking social contact, especially with other women."[11] As we have seen, fight-or-flight releases stress hormones into the system producing a pernicious and debilitating effect over time. In the tend-and-befriend response, researchers found higher levels of the hormone oxytocin working in concert with other natural opioids, such as endorphins. Animals and people with high levels of oxytocin are calmer, more relaxed, more social, and less anxious. It may be uncomfortable for some men to take in, but the message is clear. If men want to improve the odds for living a longer, healthier, and happier life, they need to develop their feminine side.

When men get overly busy with work, friendships are often the first thing they tend to drop. We need to understand that it is a mistake, having serious implications for both our health and longevity.

CHICKEN SOUP, RED WINE, AND HELPING OTHERS

An interesting study at the National Institutes of Health found that, although chicken soup may provide soothing relief to cold symptoms, it is the kindness of the loved one who brings the soup that contains the medicine.[12] The same may be true of wine. Science has found that drinking one to three glasses of red wine per day is good for the heart. While red wine does possess beneficial antioxidants, it appears that sharing friendship over a glass of wine is what makes our hearts healthier. People who typically drink one to three glasses of wine usually do so with friends. Here is another interesting finding: helping others has a greater positive effect on longevity than being helped.[13] It turns out that giving is actually receiving amplified. People thank us for our help, but in truth we should thank them for the opportunity to extend our lives a few more years.

MIRROR NEURONS

The neural network most responsible for achieving our state of connectedness is the mirror neuron system. This cluster of nerve cells was discovered in 1996 by Giaccamo Rizzollati and a team of neuroscientists at the University of Parma in Italy in an experiment conducted on macaque monkeys. They observed on brain scans that a specific cluster of brain cells fired in the frontal lobe of a monkey when it grabbed a peanut. The curious thing was that in another monkey, who was watching the first monkey grab the peanut, the same cluster of cells fired. The cells seemed to reflect the actions of the other monkey almost like a mirror reflects one's image. As the researchers investigated further, it became easy for them to predict which specific neurons would fire based on the activity performed by one monkey and observed by another. Rizzollati dubbed this cluster of cells mirror neurons.

In humans, the mirror neuron system is much more complex and appears to shape our interpersonal experiences. This mirroring is the neural mechanism by which we can read the minds of other people and empathize with them.[14] "Mirror neurons suggest that we pretend to be in another person's mental shoes," stated Marco Iacoboni of UCLA School of Medicine. "In fact, with mirror neurons we do not have to pretend; we practically are in another person's mind."[15] Daniel Goleman, author of *Emotional Intelligence*, wrote in an essay that appeared in the *New York Times*:

> *Mirror neurons track the emotional flow, movement, and even intentions of the person we are with, and replicate this sensed state in our own brain by stirring in our brain the same areas active in the other person.*
>
> *Mirror neurons offer a neural mechanism that explains emotional contagion, the tendency of one person to catch the feelings of another, particularly if strongly expressed. This brain-to-brain link may also account for feelings of rapport, which research finds depend in part on extremely rapid synchronization of people's posture, vocal pacing, and movements as they interact.[16]*

Goleman points out that mirror neurons work both ways. My hostility bumps up your blood pressure; your nurturing love lowers mine. Biologically, friends are healing, enemies are toxic.

John Cacioppo of the University of Chicago has shown that the emotional quality of our primary relationships plays a significant role in cardiovascular and endocrine function.[17] In other words, the quality of our presence has a biological impact. The more we are sensitive to our own emotions, reasoning, intentions, and body language, the better we are at reading the mind of another person. In theory, when two or more minds feel connected, when they become integrated, it means that the neural firing of one matches that of the other. It is called resonance, which means that they are biologically and psychologically joined through the ebb and flow of shifting emotions, sensations, and thoughts, extended and received, over the course of communication. They read each other more accurately and thus are able to respond more appropriately. They are more empathic, more understanding, and make sense to one another. Thus, they achieve greater coherence in their communication. It is the level of communication that builds powerful human relationships at every level of human experience, from husbands and wives to children and parents, from doctors and patients to leaders and teams.

In evolving mirror neurons, nature made the quality of our presence powerful, biologically as well as psychologically. If the quality of one's presence is fearful, things are likely to go poorly. Theoretically, if another's presence is dynamically peaceful, this clear state will be mirrored in the brain of the one who was afraid and can serve as a calming influence. It can create a sense of safety in the other and quell the emotional brain's tendency to perceive threat and to overreact.

JACK AND JILL: MIRROR NEURONS AT WORK

To dramatize how mirror neurons might work in everyday life, imagine a conversation between Jack and Jill, both of whom have potentially opposing views on the same issue. Imagine that each has an unconditional positive regard for the other; that both are skillful at locating their inner experience, staying in touch with it; and that both place a high value on listening.

Jill begins by making her argument for the direction she wants to take. As she speaks, she notices—and then ignores—an acceleration of her heart rate, the moistening of her palms with sweat, and her arms folded across her chest. Jack, who usually holds the intention of attuning himself to others, registers her affect and thinks Jill is either determined to win this argument or is fearful of losing it. He looks into her eyes and intuits fear, which generates a feeling of fear in Jack as concomitant mirror neurons fire in his brain. His fear flickers below his awareness and settles into an impatient agitation. The next thought his anxiety churns out is, *women are too emotional,* followed by the prediction that this meeting is going to take longer than he'd hoped. His impatience blends into his tone of voice, his body language, and his facial expression. He thinks he has disguised it, but it all registers in Jill's brain. As it does, she tightens her folded arms around her chest.

Jack senses her defensiveness and takes a breath. In the wider space that the breath opens, he sees the conflict that is brewing emotionally. He chooses empathy and in the next breath relaxes his thoughts, consciously drops his impatience, and tunes in to listening better. *This issue is more important to her than I thought,* he thinks. For the moment, he subordinates his considerations about the issue in favor of generating an atmosphere of safety for connecting. As Jill continues, she registers the shift in Jack and recognizes that he is genuinely listening to her. She wonders if she can trust it. But before she knows it, her attitude matches Jack's openness. She is now able to notice her anxiety and let it go. This, in turn, registers with Jack, who feels relieved, and he smiles faintly. This makes Jill smile, who stops in her discourse and with spontaneous affection, says, "By the way, Jack, good morning. How was your weekend?" "Good," he answers, and they both laugh, in part at having dodged an emotional bullet.

ACHIEVING RESONANCE

Achieving resonance takes a personal commitment to developing interpersonal intelligence. It also takes patience, trust, and awareness to ride the waves of resonance and dissonance. The approach that maps to the way mirror neurons achieve resonance is the person-centered approach, formulated by Carl R. Rogers, PhD. It is one of the most scientifically validated approaches in psychology and earned Rogers a nomination for the Nobel Peace Prize. The essential conditions for communication prescribed by this approach are now at the center of nearly every form of psychotherapy—from cognitive behavior therapy to positive psychology to Freudian analysis—and the approach has been widely applied in business, conflict resolution, community building, and educational theory.

For Rogers, one's own view of humanity is crucial in promoting the sense of connection between people. It is the foundation upon which meaningful relationships are built. Rogers's clinical experience taught him that, given the proper conditions for growth, human nature reveals itself as positive, constructive, and forward moving. This is contrary to the Calvinistic view that man is basically flawed, with an evil predisposition. It was Rogers's view that "individuals have within themselves vast resources for self-understanding and for altering their self-concepts, basic attitudes, and self-directed behavior; these resources can be tapped if a definable climate of facilitative attitudes can be provided."[18]

THREE INDISPENSABLE CONDITIONS FOR RESONANCE

Rogers formulated three conditions that must be present in order to create a climate of growth and resonance. These conditions apply in any and all relationships, whether they are therapist and client, parent and child, leader and group, teacher and student, or management and staff.[19] The conditions apply, in fact, in any situation in which the development of the person is a goal.

1. Genuineness

The first condition is genuineness, realness, or congruence. The more a person is himself in the relationship, presenting no professional front or personal facade, the greater the likelihood of constructive change and growth. This requires that we be aware of and open to the feelings and attitudes flowing within us as we relate to another. The term *transparent* catches the essence of this condition: we are willing to make ourselves transparent to the other person so the other person can clearly see what we are in the relationship. There is no holding back. What we are experiencing is available to awareness, can be lived in the relationship, and can be communicated. Thus, for Rogers, there is a close matching, or congruence, between what is being experienced at the gut level, what is present in awareness, and what is expressed.

2. Acceptance

The second attitude of importance in creating a climate for connection is acceptance and caring, or what Rogers called unconditional positive regard. When we are experiencing a positive, acceptant attitude toward whatever the other person is at that moment, connection, movement, and change are more likely to occur. We are willing for the other person to be whatever immediate feeling she is experiencing, whether confusion, resentment, fear, anger, courage, love, or pride. We value the other in a total rather than a conditional way.

3. Empathic Understanding

The third facilitative aspect of the relationship is empathic understanding. Being empathic is to perceive the point of view of another with accuracy, along with its emotional components and meanings. It means to sense the hurt or the pleasure of another as he senses it and to perceive the causes of the feelings as he perceives them. It is to enter another's private world so completely that we lose all desire to evaluate and judge it. It is to catch not only those meanings that are obvious but also those meanings which are only implicit—which he sees only dimly or as confusion. "This kind of sensitive, active listening is exceedingly rare in our lives," Rogers stated. "We think we listen, but very rarely do we listen with real understanding, true empathy. Yet listening, of this very special kind, is one of the most potent forces for change that I know."[20]

Resonance proceeds from an accepting, empathic, and honest way of being in a relationship. This way of relating arises naturally in the absence of judging, advising, admonishing, ordering, or directing. It helps us to get in touch with our actual feelings and experiences so we can become more real, less distorted, and ultimately achieve a close match between the person we strive to be and the person we are. Resonance means we are alive in the present moment, attuned to its ebbs and flows, open to a state of becoming; rather than being fixed on who or what we think we should be, or how another person should be.

$$\circ \quad \circ \quad \circ$$

How does this climate of resonance bring about personal and interpersonal growth? It maps back to mirror neurons. Rogers stated that "as persons are accepted and prized, they tend to develop a more caring attitude toward themselves." Our acceptance mirrors as self-acceptance. "As persons are empathetically heard, it becomes possible for them to listen more accurately to the flow of inner experiencings." Our listening mirrors as self-understanding. "As a person understands and prizes self," Rogers asserted, "the self becomes more congruent with their own experiencing. The person thus becomes more real, more genuine." Our willingness to be authentic in our relationships mirrors in others the freedom to be authentically who they are.[21]

When all three attitudes are present in a relationship, resonance is inevitable. Rogers's research showed that it maps to more positive, constructive, and sustainable relationships. Ironically, it proves true in the military. In an analysis of U.S. Naval Commands, researchers concluded that: "The most effective leaders in the United States Navy are warmer, more outgoing, emotionally expressive, dramatic, and sociable."[22]

Rogers acknowledged that achieving these three conditions is not always easy. Our commitment to relate in this way emerges first from a personal experience of its power to enhance our lives at every level. We build this experience as we override the tendency to judge, attack, defend, or hide behind a façade. As our relationships deepen and grow more constructive, so does our motivation to relate in this new way. The value of being genuine, empathic, and unconditionally positive in our regard for others becomes obvious, building the resolve to correct to these three conditions when we fail. And we will fail.

FORGIVENESS

We fail at offering this quality of relationship more often than we may admit; and others fail us. Often, it is because of stress, which means we are experiencing some form of fear. We are capable of making serious mistakes when fearful, reacting in ways that are hurtful and harmful, despite our initial intention. Nature wired us for fear, threat, and fight-or-flight to help us survive a dangerous world. Nature also wired us for love, empathy, and connection for the same reason.

At times, the tension between love and fear can produce a split mind leading to a divided self. In this divided state, it is inevitable that people will sometimes disappoint, betray, and fail us, and we them. This is why forgiveness is strategically important in life—biologically, socially, and psychologically. It provides a way of erasing the past. Without it, we imprison ourselves in conflict and fear, anger and hate, distrust and disconnection. These are intense emotions and, when combined, they darken our hearts and damage our brains. We hang on to an unforgiving stance because we believe it protects us. It is a delusion. Biologically, it is tantamount to taking poison and expecting the other person to die.

Why Is It So Difficult?

So why do we find it so difficult to forgive? Probably, the number one reason is we believe the person who injured us deserves our anger and punishment. This is followed by the fear that forgiving opens the door to being hurt again. Some of us even think that forgiving condones the act. We can delude ourselves into thinking our unwillingness to forgive maintains control over the injuring party. In truth, the refusal to forgive is a painful state of mind that controls us, and robs us of peace, happiness, and connection. It can mean we have stopped trusting life. But forgiveness can restore all of these qualities. Ultimately, forgiveness is a gift we give to ourselves; it has never been about condoning poor behavior. It has always been about reclaiming our peace of mind and moving on with our lives.

You Who Are Without Sin

Sometimes, what we are unable to forgive in another is related to a similar mistake we made in the past that unconscious guilt projects onto the present. Forgiving someone for a mistake or misdeed we, too, have committed offers an opportunity to release ourselves from past guilt.

Forgive but Never Forget

I have heard some people say, "I forgive, but I never forget." If we hold on to the past as we look upon a person we have theoretically forgiven, we will be unable to perceive the person as he is now. If the person who harmed us has grown from the mistake, we will fail to recognize any change in him. We will see only the image we made in pain and condemnation. This is not forgiveness. It means we cherish our old judgment of this person more than we do him. It means we cherish the past more than the present. It means our mind is still looking over its shoulder rather than moving on. Complete forgiveness means that we perceive the other person with new eyes that no longer see the past.

None of this is to say that forgiving is always easy. It is a process of healing that can take time. Serious breaches and crimes can cause a form of post-traumatic stress, in which the painful event is triggered over and over in the mind. At times, it can seem there is nothing we can do to stop it. It can be difficult to quiet the tendency to ruminate, chewing on the details, distorting facts, and imagining worst-case scenarios. At some point, though, we realize that we have become the source of our own suffering and that the price of holding on to the wrong is not worth it.

Forgiving the Unforgivable

Some people think that there are crimes that are unforgivable. It may be true. Again, what we are after, even more than a changed view of someone else, is freedom from pain and restoration of our peace of mind. When we face a particularly egregious wrong, we can take courage in the strength of others who have forgiven the unforgivable. I have a very dear friend named Zalinda who forgave the man who murdered her son. Reaching forgiveness was a long and painful process. For ten years, hardly a day passed that Zalinda did not carry the anger and hate for the murderer, along with the grief of losing her son. It was a heavy burden that began to take a toll on her health, eventually damaging her gastrointestinal system, to the point that it required surgery.

One day, her emotional pain reached a bottom and she found a willingness to find a way to heal. To her dismay, the solution that kept coming to mind was meeting the young man who had murdered her son. Eventually, Zalinda gave in and made her request. The man agreed and a series of supervised meetings were arranged at the prison. Her family and community chastised her for the decision. Her decision recycled the fear and anger people felt toward the crime.

At the first meeting, the warden even ordered a general lockup. The first few sessions were white-knuckle encounters. My friend unloaded all her hostility and contempt for this man. She expressed, in expletives, the anger she had been holding all those years. The young man did not defend himself. He listened and at times hung his head in shame. Gradually, they settled into communicating constructively, and my friend could feel the young man's remorse. The murder had happened in a drug stupor, and my friend could see it was a tragic, irreparable mistake that had ruined this young man's life, as well as her own. Zalinda eventually met separately with his parents, and felt their pain and sorrow. It shifted her. She wanted the pain to end, for everyone.

To her astonishment, Zalinda began to care for the plight of this young man, to feel compassion for him, and eventually a friendship developed between them. On one visit, during a casual moment, my friend recounted a story about her murdered son, when he was a boy. She had been in the backyard, supervising an activity with her Cub Scout den, and her son, in a show of masculine prowess, climbed the tree, grabbed the rope swing, and launched himself with the cry of Tarzan. Unfortunately, the rope was not firmly tied to the branch and he came spiraling to the ground, breaking his arm. "You should have seen the look of shock on his face when he realized the rope was loose," Zalinda told the young prisoner. Then, she paused for a moment in astonishment, with the sudden realization that she had crossed a bridge into healing "Do you realize what just happened?" she said. "We are sharing about my son, and it is all right."

Zalinda went on to advocate for the man's freedom and picked him up at the prison the day he was released. He has gone on to lead a productive life. He married and had a child. Zalinda also went on to rebuild her life, remarried, and lives in a lovely home at the edge of the sea. She will tell you that if she had not found the willingness to forgive, she would not be alive today.

The following exercise can be helpful in forgiving a person who has hurt or harmed you, and it can also be used to help you forgive yourself for a mistake you may have made but have yet to heal from.

Release[23]

Bring to mind someone who is difficult for you to forgive: a person who wronged you in some way; a person you do not like, or maybe you even hate; someone with whom you might actively avoid making contact but whose misdeed still haunts your thoughts.

1. Try to perceive light somewhere in this person—a small glimmer, one which you had not noticed.

2. Look until you see some little spark of brightness shining through the painful picture that you hold.

3. Then let this light extend until it covers the person and makes the painful picture of the person appear brighter and kinder.

4. Silently repeat to yourself the following words: I forgive you. I release you to your highest good. I free myself from this grievance and all the pain that has come from it. I release the present from the past and free my future.[24]

When you complete the exercise, reverse it. Identify a mistake or misdeed which you committed and have not yet forgiven. Apply the same process as you did in forgiving another, except now you are the subject. Perceive the light in you. Let this light extend until it covers you and makes the painful picture dissolve. Forgive yourself. Release yourself to your highest good. Let go of this mistake and all its pain. Nothing teaches the value of forgiveness as much as when we are in need of it for a mistake we have made.

When you have concluded both exercises, read the poem below by Hafiz, a Persian poet from the fourteenth century. As you read the poem, hold in your mind the knowledge that heart disease is the number one killer of Americans. Remember the villagers of Roseto, their way of connecting that created a strong community, and how it became a force that made them immune to heart disease. Remember that nature wired you for deep and meaningful relationships. Remember the three indispensable conditions, formulated by Carl Rogers, that help us reach resonance in our relationships.

It happens all the time in heaven,
And some day
It will begin to happen again on earth,
That men and women who are married,
And men and men who are Lovers,
And women and women who give each other Light,
Often will get down on their knees
And while so tenderly
Holding their lover's hand,
With tears in their eyes,
Will sincerely speak, saying,
"My dear, how can I be more loving to you?
How can I be more kind?"

12

The Fourth Quality of Mystic Cool: The Whole that Transcends the Fragments

Do not hide your light under a bushel.

The Sermon on the Mount

The fourth quality of Mystic Cool is wholeness. Wholeness is loving yourself just the way you are. It is loving life just the way it is. It is the affirmation and acceptance of the man or woman you are and are becoming, encompassing the whole of you—your failures and successes, your strengths and weaknesses, your joys and sorrows, your positive qualities and those that are not so positive. Wholeness is a sense of perfection emerging from the imperfections. It is an authentic moment in which the authentic person that is you is felt by you, opens wide in you, and is welcomed into the heart of all that is. Five seconds of this feeling is enough to transform a life.

Our authentic self is found right here, right now, through our openness to our immediate experience, whatever that experience may be. If we judge, reject, or feel conflict with our present experience, the sense of wholeness will instantly splinter and fragment. Fault finding obstructs the experience of wholeness, eventually calcifying into the belief that we are not good enough. We underestimate our strengths and undervalue our worth. We end up feeling separate, alone, inadequate. We develop a slavish concern for the expectations and evaluations of others. It reaches the point that we have no sense of our own strengths and talents, and no awareness of who we really are.

THE RED-PENCIL WORLD

Most, if not all, of us have been conditioned to be fault finders. It is a kind of cultural virus that has infected us. Fault finding springs from the age-old belief that humankind is, by nature, flawed and untrustworthy. This notion is ingrained in nearly every institution in the world, in every strata of society—in family, religion, government, education, and workplace. We were all reared in a red-pencil world, and it has shaped us. This red-pencil coercion had such a deterring effect on Albert Einstein that after he had passed his final examination, he found the consideration of any scientific problems distasteful to him for an entire year. Einstein said: "It is, in fact, nothing short of a miracle that the modern methods of instruction have not yet entirely strangled the holy curiosity of inquiry; for this delicate little plant, aside from stimulation, stands mainly in need of freedom. Without this, it goes to wrack and ruin without fail."

One cannot help but wonder how many potential contributions to humanity have been crushed beneath the wheel of capitulation. We believe an oxymoron that says we fortify strengths by focusing attention on weaknesses. Meanwhile, it is our innate strengths that grow weak. What once had heart for us inevitably withers from the depleting effects of fault finding as, increasingly, we feel ourselves losing touch with the strength of our inborn talent, curiosity, interests, and passions. Our strengths, not our weaknesses, have power to point us in the direction of the unique contribution we are here to make.

It is not uncommon today to hear people refer to themselves as recovering Christians, recovering Jews, or, in Einstein's case, as a recovering graduate student. I once worked with a group of unemployed people who dubbed themselves recovering dot-comers. In using this term, people are essentially addressing the recovery of freedom. They are referring to a process of freeing themselves from the negative view and limited thinking of their social conditioning. These people are often recovering from an ingrained view of self as flawed, guilty, inadequate, or unworthy. They are courageously reclaiming the right to follow the beat of their own drum. Often, they have come through a crisis or sea change that demanded inner strength. Inner strength is usually the only resource these people had left to meet the crisis. As they faced their dilemma, their belief was that inner strength was not going to be enough to get them through. They ended up surprising themselves. Through their ordeal, they tapped an essential quality of being—of inner strength and resourcefulness—that proved reliable, trustworthy, and effective. They discovered that what they are is good enough, when they are open to it. This quality of openness is the flow out of which our sense of wholeness emerges. Our basic nature thrives on self-direction and becomes a power with self-understanding.

This basic assumption that human nature is flawed and untrustworthy was prevalent in psychology for nearly a hundred years. In *Civilization and Its Discontent*, Sigmund Freud stated: "Our mind ... is no peacefully self-contained unity. It is rather to be compared to a modern state in which a mob, eager for enjoyment and destruction, has to be held down forcibly by a prudent superior class."[1]

Carl R. Rogers and Abraham Maslow proposed a school of psychology based on the assumption that human nature is trustworthy.[2] It was their view that human beings were innately self-correcting, self-directed, and forward moving. They hypothesized that human beings possess a directional tendency aimed at complete development, meaning the full realization of their abilities, talents, aptitudes, and strengths. Maslow called it the self-actualizing tendency, and Rogers called it the formative tendency. Rogers's assertion was the direct opposite of Freud's. He affirmed that "man's behavior is exquisitely rational, moving with subtle and ordered complexity towards the goals his or her organism is endeavoring to achieve."[3] To illustrate this formative tendency directed toward complete development, Rogers told the story of his parents' potato bin:

I remember that in my boyhood the potato bin in which we stored our winter supply of potatoes was in the basement, several feet below a small basement window. The conditions were unfavorable, but the potatoes would begin to sprout—pale white sprouts, so unlike the healthy green shoots they sent up when planted in the soil in the spring. But these sad, spindly sprouts would grow two or three feet in length as they reached toward the distant light of the window. They were, in their bizarre, futile growth, a sort of desperate expression of the directional tendency ... They would never become a plant, never mature, never fulfill their real potentiality. But under the most adverse circumstances they were striving to become. Life would not give up, even if it could not flourish. In dealing with clients whose lives have been terribly warped, in working with men and women on the back wards of state hospitals, I often think of those potato sprouts. So unfavorable have been the conditions in which these people have developed that their lives often seem abnormal, twisted, scarcely human. Yet the directional tendency in them is to be trusted. The clue to understanding their behavior is that they are striving, in the only way available to them, to move toward growth, toward becoming. To us the results may seem bizarre and futile, but they are life's desperate attempt to become itself.[4]

What I am is good enough if I would only be it openly.
Carl R. Rogers, PhD

Rogers went on to test and validate his theory of a formative tendency. We can now take it for granted. We are inherently whole, possess vast inner resources, and, in a defined attitudinal climate, we are capable of actualizing our full potential. We are capable of creating the good life.

ROGERS'S IDEA OF THE GOOD LIFE

Carl R. Rogers added his own idea to Aristotle's good life. "This process of the good life is not, I am convinced," Rogers wrote, "a life for the faint-hearted. It involves the stretching and growing of becoming more and more of one's potentialities. It involves the courage to be. It means launching oneself fully into the stream of life." For Rogers, the good life is not any fixed state. It is not a condition of acquired virtue or contentment or nirvana or happiness. It is not a condition in which the individual is necessarily fulfilled or actualized or even well-adjusted. "The good life," he wrote, "is a *process*, not a state of being. It is a direction, not a destination. It is the direction we choose for ourselves, when there is the psychological freedom to move in *any* direction."[5]

The Fully Functioning Person

Rogers also formulated what he called the fully functioning person. This is a person who has transcended the red-pencil world of suffocating conformity and fault finding. It is a person who has come to trust in his own organism, and thus is less invested in the approval or sanction of an external authority, and is more reliant on the authority of his own creative nature and strength. It is a person whose sense of wholeness arises from an openness to his own experience, whatever that may be.

> To be nobody-but-yourself—in a world that is doing its best,
> night and day, to make you everybody else—means to fight
> the hardest battle which any human being can fight,
> and never stop fighting.
>
> e.e. cummings

The Self As Whole

Wholeness depends on a willingness to listen to ourselves, to experience what is going on within, to feel it, and to move from it and with it. It is an acceptance of whatever we feel in the moment—from fear and sorrow and disappointment to passion and kindness and awe. "One way of expressing the fluidity which is present in such existential living," Rogers wrote, "is to say that the self and personality emerge *from* experience rather than experience being translated or twisted to fit preconceived self-structure."[6]

STRENGTH FINDING

How do we become a fully functioning person? First, by quieting the tendency to find fault so we can begin to acknowledge our strengths. It is a muscle we need to develop. Research shows that we are poor at identifying strengths but quick to name our faults. Herb Otto, who conducted research on human potential at the universities of Georgia and Utah in the 1960s, found that people minimize their strengths by brushing off positive attributes and holding to a narrow view of their talents and skills. We tend to deflect, deny, dismiss, and discount positive feedback.

Disowning Our Strengths—The 4 Ds

Deflect it	Dismiss it
• Giving credit to someone else	• Changing the subject
Deny it	**Discount it**
• Denying our part was valuable	• "It's no big deal"

Things haven't improved in the last fifty years since Otto's research. The Gallup Organization, in conducting psychological profiles with [nearly] two million individuals in 101 companies, came to the same conclusion. They found that "most of us have little sense of our talents and strengths, much less the ability to build our lives around them. Instead, guided by our parents, by our teachers, by our managers, and by psychology's fascination with pathology, we become experts in our weaknesses and spend our lives trying to repair these flaws, while our strengths lie dormant and neglected."[7] The study was presented in Marcus Buckingham and Donald Clifton's bestseller *Now Discover Your Strengths.* One of the questions asked was, "At work, do you have the opportunity to do what you do best every day?" Just twenty percent answered positively. The study also found that the longer an employee stays with an organization and the higher he or she climbs the career ladder, the more negative the response to the question. Gallup also found that businesses that increased the number of employees using their strengths and talent, "saw . . . increases in productivity, customer loyalty, and employee retention."[8] They found that "the most effective people are those who understand their strengths. The data show that these people are best able to develop strategies to meet and exceed the demands of their daily lives, careers, and their families."[9] Sadly, these people are few in number.

Herb Otto found that acknowledging one's strengths, was the single biggest factor in building self-esteem. Yet we tend to shy away from acknowledgments, confusing a recognition of strength with a lack of humility. It is a false humility. Certainly, it is arrogant to compare our innate talents to those of others and then to dismiss these people as less than us. The truth is, more often than not, we compare ourselves to others and see ourselves as the lesser. Yet we do not see this as equally arrogant.

○   ○   ○

"Our deepest fear," stated Marianne Williamson in *A Return to Love,* "is not that we are inadequate. Our deepest fear is that we are powerful beyond measure. It is our light, not our darkness, that most frightens us."[10] The Trappist monk Thomas Merton echoed that sentiment: "Perhaps I am stronger than I think," he wrote. "Perhaps I am even afraid of my strength and turn it against myself, thus making myself weak. . . . Perhaps I am most afraid of the strength of God in me."[11] It is as if we are hiding the light of our strength under a bushel. We can begin to lift the bushel by canceling the fault-finding, red-pencil mindset in favor of an attitude of strength finding. We can affirm for ourselves that we possess an inherent self-actualizing tendency that is programmed to reach complete development. We can begin to trust it.

BECOMING A STRENGTH FINDER[12]

Becoming a strength finder is simple. It begins with quieting the voice that says we are not good enough. The best indicator of strength is the fire it lights in our hearts whenever we exercise it.

1. Make a list of at least five of your strengths. Write them down.

2. Pick one strength and, starting tomorrow, commit the morning to strengthening it by becoming familiar with the various ways you can use it.

3. As you use it, acknowledge its value.

4. In the afternoon, commit to seeing one strength in another person and acknowledging it, at first quietly to yourself, and then openly to the other person.

5. Identify three people who are attuned to your strengths, and use the relationships to affirm you.

Take small steps at first, weaving your strength into other functions you perform. Then commit to growing this strength by gradually increasing it, this week, the week after, and the week after that, until you begin to feel it growing what is best in you.

In workshops I conduct with companies,[13] we do an exercise called Strength Finding. We divide people into groups of eight. We place one person in what we call the warm seat. Another person is designated as the scribe. Then, in round-robin fashion, each person in the group states a strength she sees in the person occupying the warm seat. Each person in the group is exposed to several rounds of positive feedback. On a piece of paper, the scribe records the responses. We repeat the exercise until everyone in the group has sat in the warm seat.

At the outset, when we explain to participants the process we are about to do, nearly everyone groans, or laughs nervously, or squirms in his or her seat. Yet, as the rounds proceed, it becomes easier and easier for people to give thoughtful, sincere acknowledgements to the person in the warm seat. It is touching to see the care people give to the process. Often, a person sits in quiet for a moment, until they find the exact words to express a genuine sentiment. Invariably, the face of the person being praised is flushed with embarrassment.

As a trainer, I see, firsthand, what the research reveals: that we have real difficulty acknowledging or being acknowledged for our strengths. At times, I have to encourage the uncomfortable person in the warm seat to resist the impulse to block out the compliment. But as the exercise moves forward, the feeling in the room lifts. By the conclusion, after everyone has had a turn, the room seems to fill with a mysterious light, and the positive energy is palpable. Smiles abound, here and there people placed a hand on the shoulder of another, and everyone feels great. This Strength Finding exercise is one of the first things people refer to, months later in follow-up debriefings, as something they remembered as land-mark in the training. Some have even implemented it in their families with great results.

John F. Kennedy wanted America to "think of education as the means of developing our greatest abilities, because," he stated, "in each of us there is a private hope and dream which, fulfilled, can be translated into benefit for everyone and greater strength for our nation."[15] Marcus Buckingham, coauthor of *Now, Discover Your Strengths* and author of *One Thing You Need to Know*, counsels us to "find a tiny stream in which [our] strengths can flow, and carve it into the Mississippi."[16]

Epilogue:
Never, Never, Never Give Up

I always entertain great hopes.

Robert Frost

We have all tried to get by without giving much attention to our peace of mind. We have not quite understood its power or what it means to cherish ourselves and one another. Individually, and as a species, we have not quite understood what Mother Teresa meant when she said if we have no peace it is because we have forgotten that we belong to each other. Our lack of understanding has now brought us to a crossroads, just as it did fifty thousand years ago, when we finally understood the creative power of the neocortex, after failing to use it for eighty thousand years.[1] Then suddenly, our genius miraculously emerged with a surge in ingenuity. Egypt, Athens, Rome, Harappa, and the Imperial City suddenly rose from the sand, and shortly thereafter, we were walking on the moon. If, fifty thousand years ago, the sudden surge of ingenuity had not occurred, Homo sapiens would not have survived. But we woke up in time. One by one our ancestors changed the world by tapping the creative power that was dawning in their brains. Step by step they created small changes that led to larger results, until the difference was everywhere.

Epilogue

THE DAWNING OF A NEW AGE

We need to wake up again. We are, once more, at another crossroad of survival, in need of a second surge of collective genius to save us. We are challenged to change the world by tapping the power of higher consciousness. We are challenged to tap the genius of peace. Fortunately, the neural circuitry is in place to do so.

How do we activate this neural power? We strengthen the power of peace by choosing it every day, in small and large ways. In the words of Mahatma Gandhi, "we must become the change we want to see in the world." We can do this by letting go of fear, in whatever form it takes. We can let go of the past and live each moment as a new one. We can extend unconditional regard and compassion to our fellow man. We can strengthen the willingness to forgive. We can learn to value our own strengths, to use them by stretching ourselves, and to encourage the strengths in others. We can transcend a limited self-interest to think and act on behalf of generations to come.

Peace does not mean we will never find ourselves in a place without agitation, problems, or stress. It means choosing to be in the midst of these things, and choosing to be calm and clear minded. Peace takes practice. "Peace is a daily, a weekly, a monthly process," John F. Kennedy once stated, "gradually changing opinions, slowly eroding old barriers, quietly building new structures."[2]

GOING IN THE RIGHT DIRECTION

There will be the inevitable setbacks when fearful thinking activates negative emotions. The old imagined threats will raise their heads again, sending mind and body into an uproar and triggering the old, unfortunate behaviors. There will be days when everything will seem to go wrong and other days when we are staggered by bad news. At times, the pull of the storm will be strong. Take heart. If we make mistakes, we can forgive ourselves and choose once again the experience we want. Ralph Waldo Emerson counseled:

Epilogue

Finish each day and be done with it. You have done what you could. Some blunders and absurdities no doubt crept in; forget them as soon as you can. Tomorrow is a new day; begin it well and serenely, with too high a spirit to be encumbered with your old nonsense. This day is all that is good and fair. It is too dear, with its hopes and invitations, to waste a moment on yesterdays.

"What we demonstrate today, tomorrow, and the next day," stated Ernest Holmes, "is not as important as the tendency which our thought is taking ... the dominant attitude of our mind." If everyday things are a little better, a little more harmonious, a little more health giving and joyous; if each day we are expressing more life, we are going in the right direction.[3]

If You're Stuck, Imagine a Door

Some ingrained patterns, of course, are stronger than others. They can seem as though they will always overwhelm and defeat us, and we might believe there is no escaping them. Dr. Gerald Jampolsky, the father of attitudinal healing, suggests using active imagination to counter them. In his classic *Love Is Letting Go of Fear*, he offered a visualization that can be very effective:

Picture a wall and let it represent your problem. On the wall, paint a door and hang a red exit sign above it that says, The Way to Freedom. Imagine yourself opening the door, walking through it, and shutting it firmly behind you. Your problem is no longer with you since you have left it behind. Experience the newfound freedom by imagining yourself in a place where you have no worries, no stress, and everything you do gives you joy. When you are ready to leave your happy retreat, bring with you this newly found sense of release from past problems. In the freshness of your new perception, solutions previously unavailable to you will now occur.[4]

177

Epilogue

Victory Is Assured

"No matter what is going on, never give up," counsels His Holiness the Dalai Lama. "Work for peace, in your heart and in the world. And I say

again, never give up."[5] Victory is assured if we do not give up. Eventually, new experiences will greet us if we practice. There is no greater motivation than good results, and there is no greater result than a peaceful life.

This book has presented tools that can help make the shift at a personal level. It is meant as a guide. Each tool addresses fear, the stress it causes, and the illusions that underlie most of our fears. Each works in shifting fear to peace. It is not necessary for you to master each and every tool. Use whichever tools work for you, but use them to bring peace to your life and to the world. In the Addendum that follows, there is a simple practice that can get you started.

I wish you peace, every day, all day long.

Addendum:
A Simple Practice

GETTING STARTED

1. Begin each day in quiet—as soon as possible—after waking. Read the Watching the Thinker tool on page 128 before beginning. Duration is not the major concern. If this exercise begins to feel difficult, continue a minute or two more. You may find the difficulty eases and drops away. If not, it's time to stop. Conclude each sitting by reading Attributes of a Dynamically Peaceful Attitude on page 115.

2. Try using the Clear Button exercise on page 129 throughout the day to stop stressful, fearful thinking at the point of inception.

3. Read the Transcending the Background of Negativity tool on page 102 and commit to practicing the tool every day for two weeks.

4. Choose one of the tasks from the list on page 181, titled "It's in the Small Stuff," and perform a different one each day until you have done them all.

Addendum: A Simple Practice

USING TOOLS TO TRANSCEND STRESS, NEGATIVITY AND ADVERSITY

1. Whenever stress is escalating in you, ask yourself, what am I afraid of? Become adept at doing this. Reread the What Am I Afraid Of exercise on page 100 and practice shifting your fearful, stressful thinking with the Refuting Fear with Reality tool on page 100.

2. If you face an encounter that has typically been stressful for you in the past, such as a meeting with a person you perceive as an adversary, use the PreAttitude tool on page 145 to reframe your attitude.

3. If you make a mistake that activates negative self-talk, use the Refuting the Critical Voice tool on page 134.

4. If you need to forgive someone or yourself, use the Release tool on page 163.

TRACK YOUR GROWING POWER THROUGH AWARENESS

1. Periodically, review your Stressometer results on page 92 and Signs of Stress on pages 93. Retest yourself to see what factors are changing. The Stressometer reminds you of where stress emanates most strongly in you (mentally, emotionally, physically, or in your attitude). Signs of Stress indicates the problems that stress cause you. Take note of where you may be improving with these problems.

2. Once a month, take the Stress Test at MysticCool.com and keep track of your scores.

For the first month or so, it is helpful to review your Signs of Stress pages and the Stressometer.

It's in the Small Stuff

Choose the longest line at a store and stand in it, using your mind creatively to take advantage of the wait or to choose peace.

Look out the window for thirty seconds and let your mind go. Watch the wind blow or the sun shine or the rain fall.

Do one special thing for yourself today.

Drive home in the slow lane.

Smile more today.

Listen to calming music instead of the news on the drive home.

Practice listening without interrupting.

Buy a small gift for a friend or family member.

Call a good friend you haven't talked to in a while.

Look for the best in someone you know.

Devote today to seeing your strengths and positive qualities.

Practice forgiving trivial errors.

Use a measuring stick other than business to measure your accomplishments, such as your talents, creative abilities, human qualities, or close relationships.

Quietly do good deeds and acts of kindness.

Practice receiving compliments graciously.

Accept that life is unfinished business.

Take five minutes today to recall times when you were happy.

Commit to stop judging yourself for your lack of perfection.

Consider the notion that perfection is in the imperfections.

When you feel conflict today, tell yourself, "I am not going to let this person or situation control how I feel."

Today, feel more and think less. Become skillful at knowing how you feel by making *I feel* . . . statements.

Addendum: A Simple Practice

DURING THE DAY

If you are having a particularly stressful day, take a five-minute break and go for a walk outside using the Clear Button on page 129 to quiet stressful thinking.

At the end of a particularly stressful day, before going home, do the Feel It To Heal It process on page 96.

MYSTICCOOL.COM

A companion website at MysticCool.com has been developed to allow you to download worksheets for doing the exercises and audio files presented by Don Joseph Goewey of the guided processes in the book. Links to workshops and coaching based on Mystic Cool is also provided, as well as access to Don's Blog.

Notes

PROLOGUE

1. Rollo May, *The Meaning of Anxiety* (New York: W. W. Norton, 1997), x.

2. Søren Kierkegaard, *The Concept of Dread* (Princeton, NJ: Princeton University Press, 1944), 139.

3. Alberto Loizaga, "Buenos Aires, Argentina: Pilar," *The Journey: The Jampolsky Outreach Foundation Newsletter* (2002): 2.

4. Daniel Siegel, "Patterns of Processing" (Audio recording of lecture at IEA Conference, San Francisco, 2005).

5. Eckhart Tolle, *The Power of Now* (Novato, CA: New World Library, 2000), 122.

CHAPTER 1

1. Mokhtar H. Gado, Joseph Hanaway, and Thomas A. Woolsey, *The Brain Atlas: A Visual Guide to the Human Central Nervous System* (Hoboken: John Wiley & Sons, 2003), 4.

2. Erik Kandel, *In Search of Memory: The Emergence of a New Science of Mind* (New York: W. W. Norton, 2006), xi.

Notes

3. Hughes Medical Institute, "Evidence that Human Brain Evolution Was a Special Event," written by Howard Bruce T. Lahn, *ScienceDaily* (December 29, 2004): http://www.sciencedaily.com/releases/2005/01/050111165229.htm.

4. Princeton University, "How Did We Get So Smart? Study Sheds Light On Evolution of the Brain," *ScienceDaily* (May 10, 2001), http://www.sciencedaily.com/releases/2001/05/010510071941.htm.

5. Aristotle, *Nichomachean Ethics*, trans. W. D. Ross. (Kitchner, ON: Batoche Books, 1999), 12.

6. Haim G. Ginott, *Teacher and Child: A Book for Parents and Teachers* (New York: Collier, 1995), 15.

7. Rollo May, *The Meaning of Anxiety* (New York: W. W. Norton, 1997), 209.

8. Visit MysticCool.com to learn more about offered workshops, personal coaching, and read Don Goewey's blog for updates on events.

9. Ernest Holmes, *The Science of Mind* (New York: Dodd, Meade & Company, 1938), 47.

10. Paraphrasing of Goethe's statement. The actual statement reads: *Seize this very minute. What you can do, or dream you can do, begin it.*

11. Howard Gardner, PhD, *Frames of Mind: The Theory of Multiple Intelligences* (New York: Basic Books, 1983), 73.

12. Mihaly Csikszentmihalyi, PhD, *Flow: The Psychology of Optimal Experience* (New York: HarperCollins, 1990), 3.

13. D. H. Lawrence, "We Are Transmitters," *Selected Poems* (New York: Viking Press, 1959), 105.

14. Abraham Joshua Heschel, *I Asked for Wonder* (New York: Crossroad Publishing, 2006), 67.

15. Bruce McEwen, *The End of Stress As We Know It* (Washington, DC: Joseph Henry Press, 2002), 13.

16. The Gallup Organization, "Lifestyle Poll" (January 24, 2007).

17. American Psychological Association, "Stress in America," October 24, 2007, pg. 15, apahelpcenter.mediaroom.com/file.php/138/Stress+in+America+REPORT+FINAL.doc.

Notes

18. Visit MysticCool.com to learn more about offered workshops, personal coaching, and read Don Goewey's blog for updates on events.

19. Vivienne Parry, "Stress: A Blight on Modern Life," *BBC News* (September 6, 2005).

20. Mihaly Csikszentmihalyi, PhD, *Flow: The Psychology of Optimal Experience* (New York: HarperCollins, 1990).

21. Ibid., 3.

22. Mihaly Csikszentmihalyi, PhD, *Finding Flow: The Psychology of Engagement with Everyday Life* (New York: Basic Books, 1997), 22.

Chapter 2

1. Thomas S. Collett, Emma Edwards, Helen J. Frier, Susi Neale, and Claire Smith, "Magnetic Compass Cues and Visual Pattern Learning in Honeybees," *The Journal of Experimental Biology* 199 (1996): 1353–1361.

2. Christopher Crowe and Michael Mann, *The Last of the Mohicans*, screenplay based on the novel by James Fenimore Cooper, http://www .dailyscript.com/scripts/last-of-the-mohicans-script.html.

3. W. T. Greenough and F. R. Volkmar, "Rearing Complexity Affects Branching of Dendrites in the Visual Cortex of the Rat," *Science* 176 (1972): 1445, 1447.

4. Earl K. Miller et al., "Different Time Courses of Learning-Related Activity in the Prefrontal Cortex and Striatum," *Nature* 433 (2005): 873–876.

5. A. R. Damasio, *Descartes' Error: Emotion, Reason, and the Human Brain* (New York: G. P. Putnam, 1994), 59.

6. Chris Mercogliano and Kim Debus, "The Unfolding of Intelligence: An Interview with Joseph Chilton Pearce," *Journal of Family Life* 5, no. 1 (1999): 1.

7. Ibid., 1.

8. Ibid., 2.

9. R. McCraty and D. Tomasino, "Emotional Stress, Positive Emotions, and Psychophysiological Coherence," *Stress in Health and Disease*, ed. B. B. Arnetz and R. Ekman (Berlin: Wiley-VCH, 2006): 342–365.

10. D. Tomasino. "The Psychophysiological Basis of Creativity and Intuition: Accessing 'The Zone' of Entrepreneurship," *International Journal of Entrepreneurship and Small Business* 4, no . 5 (2007): 528–542.

11. M. Atkinson, R. T. Bradley, and R. McCraty, "Electrophysiological Evidence of Intuition: The Surprising Role of the Heart, Part 1," *Journal of Alternative and Complementary Medicine* 10, no. 1 (2004): 133–143.

12. Matthew 16:3 (International Standard Version, 2008).

13. Daniel J. Siegel, MD, "Psychiatric Annals" (working draft, 2008).

14. Carl Rogers, *The Carl Rogers Reader*, ed. Howard Kirschenbaum and Valerie Land Henderson, 3rd ed. (New York: Houghton-Mifflin, 1989), 416.

15. Jean-Jacques Rousseau, *The Social Contract* (New York: Penguin Classics, 1968), 49.

16. Nikos Zanzantzakis, *Report to Greco* (New York: Simon and Schuster, 1965), 445.

17. Ibid.

18. Ibid.

19. Steve Jobs, "'You've Got to Find What You Love,' Jobs Says," Stanford University News Service (June 15, 2005), http://news-service .stanford.edu/news/2005/june15/jobs-061505.html.

CHAPTER 3

1. Abraham Lincoln, "First Inaugural Address" (March 4, 1861).

2. Daniel Siegel, MD, *The Mindful Brain* (New York: W. W. Norton & Co., 2007), 41–44.

3. C. E. Kerr, S. Lazar, R. H. Wasserman, et al., "Meditation Experience is Associated with Increased Cortical Thickness," *Neuroreport* 16 (2005): 1893–1897.

4. Andrew Cooper, *Playing in the Zone: Exploring the Spiritual Dimension of Sports* (Boston: Shambhala Publications, 1998).

5. Mihaly Csikszentmihalyi, PhD, *Flow, The Psychology of Optimal Experience* (New York: HarperCollins, 1990), 33.

Notes

6. Ralph Waldo Emerson, *Self-Reliance and Other Essays* (New York: Dover Publications, 1993), 27.

7. Jeff Hawkins, *On Intelligence* (New York: Times Books, 2004), 40.

8. Ibid., 66–67.

9. University of Rochester, "Mysterious 'Neural Noise' Actually Primes Brain for Peak Performance," written by Alex Pouge, *Science Daily* (November 13, 2006): http://www.sciencedaily.com/releases/2006/11/061112094812.htm.

10. Richard G. Klein, *The Dawn of Human Culture* (New York: Nevraumount Publishing Co., 2002), 133.

11. Doron M. Behar, Richard Villems, et al., "The Dawn of Human Matrilineal Diversity," *The American Journal of Human Genetics* 82, no. 5 (April 24, 2008): 1130–1140.

12. Gene Scheer, "American Anthem" lyrics, 1999.

13. Stanley Milgram, *Obedience to Authority* (New York: Harper-Collins, 1974), 73–88.

CHAPTER 4

1. Tennessee Williams, *Suddenly Last Summer* (New York: Dramatists Play Service, Inc., 1957), 8–9.

2. Wallace Stegner, *Wolf Willow* (New York: Penguin, 1955), 152.

3. James Brewer, Larry Cahill, John D. E. Gabrieli, Canli Turhan, and Zuo Zhao, "Event-Related Activation in the Human Amygdala Associates with Later Memory for Individual Emotional Experience," *The Journal of Neuroscience* 20, RC99 (2000): 1–5.

4. John Brockman, "Parallel Memories: Putting Emotions Back into the Brain, A Talk with Joseph LeDoux," *Edge: The Third Culture*, http://www.edge.org/documents/archive/edge7.html.

5. Willa Cather, *My Ántonia* (New York: Barnes and Noble Classics, 2005), 33.

6. Robert M. Sapolsky, *Why Zebras Don't Get Ulcers: An Updated Guide to Stress, Stress Related Diseases, and Coping*, 2nd Rev Ed. (New York: W. H. Freeman, 1998), 5.

Notes

7. Center for Neural Science at New York University, "Emotion, Memory and the Brain," LeDoux Laboratory, http://www.cns.nyu.edu/home/ledoux/index.html.

8. Joe T. Zsien, "Building a Brainier Mouse," *Scientific American* 289, no. 4 (2000): 63–69.

9. Albert Camus, *Between Hell and Reason: Essays from the Resistance Newspaper Combat, 1944-1947* (Middletown: Wesleyan, 1991), iii.

10. Federal Bureau of Investigation. Washington, DC: FBI, U.S. Department of Justice. *Crime in the United States*, 2003. Section 2, page 18, Table 2.7 entitled *Murder Victim/Offender Relationship*, (2004).

11. Michael R. Gottfredson and Travis Hirschi, *A General Theory of Crime* (Palo Alto: Stanford University Press, 1990), 32.

12. American Psychological Association, "Stress in America," October 24, 2007, pg. 5, apahelpcenter.mediaroom.com/file.php/138/Stress+in+America+REPORT+FINAL.doc.

13. G. Keinan, "Decision-Making Under Stress: Scanning of Alternatives Under Controllable and Uncontrollable Threats," *Journal of Personality and Social Psychology* 52, no. 3 (1987): 639–644.

14. Wesley E. Sime, MPH/PhD, "Stress Management: A Review of Principles," *The Health and Human Performance at the University of Nebraska* (1997): http://cehs.unl.edu/stress/workshop/tableofcontents.html.

15. D. Caroline Blanchard, Robert J. Blanchard, Ana María Magariños, Bruce S. McEwen, Christina R. McKittrick, and Randall R. Sakai, "Chronic Social Stress Reduces Dendritic Arbors in CA3 of Hippocampus and Decreases Binding to Serotonin Transporter Sites," *Synapse* 36, no. 2 (2000): 85–94.

16. Robert D. Rogers et al., "Tryptophan Depletion Alters the Decision-Making of Healthy Volunteers Through Altered Processing of Reward Cues," *Neuropsychopharmacology*, 28, no. 1 (January 2003): 153–62.

17. Emily Singer, "Tryptophan, Turkey, and Trust: Your Holiday Turkey Won't Give You More Faith in Your Family, but New Research Suggests that there Is a Relationship between Tryptophan and Trust," *Technology Review at MIT* (November 21, 2007).

Notes

18. D. C. Blanchard, R. J. Blanchard, Z. Celen, L. R. Lucas, C. Markham, B. S. McEwen, R. R. Sakai, and K. L. Tamashiro, "Repeated Exposure to Social Stress Has Long-Term Effects on Indirect Markers of Dopaminergic Activity in Brain Regions Associated with Motivated Behavior," *Neuroscience* 124, no. 2 (2004): 449–457.

19. P. Arbisi, P. Collins, R. Depue, A. Leon, and M. Luciana, "Dopamine and the Structure of Personality: Relation of Agonist-Induced Dopamine D2 Activity to Positive Emotionality," *Journal of Personality and Social Psychology* 67 (1994): 485–498.

20. American Psychological Association, "Stress in America," October 24, 2007, pg. 5, apahelpcenter.mediaroom.com/file.php/138/Stress+in+America+REPORT+FINAL.doc.

21. Ibid., 7.

22. Kari A. Barnett and Robert L. Del Campo, "Work and Family Balance Among Dual-Earner Working-Class Mexican-Americans: Implications for Therapists," *Contemporary Family Therapy* 25, no. 4 (2003): 353–366.

23. Matthew F. Bumpus and Ann C. Crouter, "Linking Parents' Work Stress to Children's and Adolescents' Psychological Adjustment," *Current Directions in Psychological Science* 10, no. 5 (2001): 156–159.

24. Jeanna Bryner, "Kids to Parents: Leave the Stress at Work," *Associated Press* (January 23, 2007).

25. American Institute of Stress, "Job Stress" (September 10, 2001): http://www.stress.org/job.htm. "Absenteeism due to job stress has escalated: According to a survey of 800,000 workers in over 300 companies, the number of employees calling in sick because of stress tripled from 1996 to 2000. An estimated 1 million workers are absent every day due to stress. The European Agency for Safety and Health at Work reported that over half of the 550 million working days lost annually in the U.S. from absenteeism are stress related and that one in five of all last minute no-shows are due to job stress."

26. S. Hawken, S. Ounpuu, S. Yusuf, et al., "Effect of Potentially Modifiable Risk Factors Associated with Myocardial Infarction in 52 Countries (The INTERHEART Study): Case-Control Study," *Lancet* 364 (2006): 937–952.

Notes

27. The Gallup Organization, "Lifestyle Poll" (January 24, 2007).

28. Lynn Franco, "U.S Job Satisfaction Declines," The Conference Board, Press Release (Febuary 23, 2007): http://www.conference-board.org/utilities/pressDetail.cfm?press_ID=3075

29. The Gallup Organization, "Lifestyle Poll" (January 24, 2007).

30. Avshalom Caspi, Andrea Danese, Maria Melchior, Barry J. Milne, Terrie E. Moffitt, and Richie Poulton, "Work Stress Precipitates Depression and Anxiety in Young, Working Women and Men," *Psychological Medicine* 37 (2007): 1119–1129.

31. Jessica Innis Baltes, André Martin, and Kyle Meddings, "The Stress of Leadership," *Leading Effectively*, The Center for Creative Leadership—A CCL Research White Paper (2007): http://www.ccl.org/leadership/enewsletter/2007/JUNissue.aspx.

32. Statistics Canada, "Work Stress Among Health Care Providers," *Health Reports* 18, no. 4 (2007): 33–36.

33. W. Dunagan, V. Fraser, T. Gallagher, J. Garbutt, E. Hazel, W. Levinson, and A. Waterman, "The Emotional Impact of Medical Errors on Practicing Physicians in the United States and Canada," *Joint Commission Journal on Quality and Patient Safety* 33, no. 8 (2007): 467–476(10).

34. M. Attridge and J. Lapp, "Worksite Interventions Reduce Stress among High School Teachers and Staff," *International Journal of Stress Management* 7, no. 3 (2000): 229–232.

35. Sherry A. Benton, Stephen L. Benton, Fred B. Newton, John M. Robertson, and Wen-Chih Tseng, "Changes in Counseling Center Client Problems Across 13 Years," *Professional Psychology: Research and Practice* 34, no. 1 (Kansas State University, 2003), 66–72.

CHAPTER 5

1. Mind and Life Institute: http://www.mindandlife.org/mission.org_section.html. The Mind and Life Institute is dedicated to fostering dialogue and research at the highest possible level between modern science and the great living contemplative traditions, especially Buddhism.

Notes

2. Michael S. Gazzaniga, *The Mind's Past* (Berkeley: University of California Press, 1998), xi.

3. L. Colucci-D'Amato, "The End of the Central Dogma of Neurobiology: Stem Cells And Neurogenesis in Adult CNS," *Neurological Sciences* 27 no. 4 (September, 2006): 266–270.

4. Carol S. Dweck, *Mindset, The New Psychology of Success* (New York: Random House, 2006), 4.

5. Sharon Begley, *Train Your Mind, Change Your Brain* (New York: Ballantine Books, 2007), 30.

6. M. Fallah, E. Fuchs, E. Gould, C. G. Gross, A. J. Reeves, and P. Tanapat, "Hippocampal Neurogenesis in Adult Old World Primates," *Proceedings of the National Academy of Science* 9 (1996): 5263–5267.

7. A. M. Alborn, T. Bjork-Eriksson, P. S. Eriksson, F. H. Gage, C. Nordborg, E. Perfilieva, and D. A. Peterson, "Neurogenesis in the Adult Human Hippocampus," *Nature Medicine* 11 (1998): 1313–1317.

8. J. P. Brasil-Neto, A. Cammarota, L. G. Cohen, M. Hallett, D. Nguyet, and A. Pascual-Leone, "Modulation of Muscle Responses Evoked by Transcranial Magnetic Stimulation during the Acquisition of New Fine Motor Skills," *Journal of Neurophysiology* 74, no. 3 (1995): 1037–1045.

9. Sharon Begley and Jeffrey Schwartz, *The Mind and the Brain* (New York: Regan Books, 2002), chapter 2.

10. Peter Bieling, Carol Garson, Kimberly Goldapple, Helen Mayberg, Sidney Kennedy, Mark Lau, and Zindel Segal, "Modulation of Cortical-Limbic Pathways in Major Depression, Treatment-Specific Effects of Cognitive Behavior Therapy," *Archives of General Psychiatry* 61, no. 1 (2004): 34–41.

11. Carey Goldberg, "Brain Mapping May Guide Treatment for Depression," *The Boston Globe* (January 6, 2006).

12. His Holiness the Dalai Lama, foreword to *Train the Mind, Change the Brain,* by Sharon Begley (New York: Ballantine Books, 2003), vii.

13. Daniel Goleman, "The Lama in the Lab," *Shambhala Sun* (March 2003): 64–72.

14. Sharon Begley, "How Thinking Can Change the Brain," *The Wall Street Journal Science Journal* (January 19, 2007): B-1.

Notes

15. Daniel Goleman, "The Lama in the Lab," *Shambala Sun* (March 2003): 64–72.

16. R. J. Davidson, J. Kabat-Zinn, et al., "Alterations in Brain and Immune Function Produced by Mindfulness Meditation," *Psychosomatic Medicine* 65 (2003): 564–570, http://psyphz.psych.wisc.edu/web/pubs/2003/alterations_by_mindfulness.pdf.

17. Daniel Goleman, "Finding Happiness: Cajole Your Brain to Lean to the Left," *The New York Times* (February 4, 2005).

18. Eckhart Tolle, *The Power of Now* (Novato, CA: New World Library, 2000), 71.

19. Daniel Goleman, "The Lama in the Lab," *Shambala Sun* (March, 2003): 64–72

20. Diane Cirincione, PhD, and Gerald Jampolsky, *Change Your Mind, Change Your Life* (New York: Bantam Books, 1993).

21. Eckhart Tolle, *The Power of Now* (Novato, CA: New World Library, 2000), 122.

22. Robert Jastrow, *The Enchanted Loom: Mind in the Universe* (New York: Touchstone, 1982), 44.

CHAPTER 6

1. Jane E. Allen, "Building Up to a Meltdown—Stress Can Kill You, and We're Beginning to Understand How," *Los Angeles Times* (June 8, 2004): C-1.

2. Research on Guided Imagery has been conducted at UC Davis Medical Center, Pennsylvania State College of Medicine, Columbia University Presbyterian Hospital, Memorial Sloan Kettering, and the Veterans Administration.

3. Jack Nicklaus, *Golf My Way* (New York: Simon and Schuster, 1974), 80.

4. Mihaly Csikszentmihalyi, PhD, *Flow: The Psychology of Optimal Experience* (New York: Harper & Row, 1990), 91.

5. Worksheets for this exercise can be downloaded at MysticCool.com.

6. Ibid.

7. Ibid.

8. Ibid.

9. Anthony de Mello, *Awareness* (New York: Doubleday, 1992), 78–83.

10. Ibid., 56–58.

11. Glen Ellen, Foundation For Inner Peace, *A Course in Miracles* (1992), 240.

CHAPTER 7

1. Larry Schwartz, "No Ordinary Joe," *ESPN.com*, (July 30, 1982): http://espn.go.com/classic/biography/s/montana_joe.html.

2. Ibid.

3. Viktor Frankl, *Man's Search for Meaning* (Boston: Beacon Press, 1992), 85.

4. Ibid., 81.

5. Ibid., 75.

6. Ibid., 50.

7. Ibid., 51.

8. Ibid., 47.

9. David Whyte, *Clear Mind, Wild Heart* (Louisville, CO: Sounds True, 2002), audiobook.

CHAPTER 8

1. José Ortega y Gasset, *The Revolt of the Masses* (New York: W. W. Norton & Co., 1993), 141.

2. Visit MysticCool.com to learn more about offered workshops, personal coaching, and read Don Goewey's blog for updates on events.

3. Mihaly Csikszentmihalyi, PhD, *Finding Flow: The Psychology of Engagement with Everyday Life* (New York: Basic Books, 1997), 19–21.

4. Daniel Siegel, MD, *The Mindful Brain* (New York: W. W. Norton & Co., 2007), 32.

5. Daniel Siegel, "Patterns of Processing," Lecture at the IEA Conference 2005, San Francisco.

Notes

6. R. Pidikiti, E. Taub, and G. Uswatte, "Constraint-Induced Movement Therapy: A New Family of Techniques with Broad Application to Physical Rehabilitation—A Clinical Review," *Journal of Rehabilitation Research and Development* 36 (1999): 237–251.

CHAPTER 9

1. Eckhart Tolle, *The Power of Now* (Novato, CA: New World Library, 2000), 71.

2. Byron Katie, *I Need Your Love—Is It True?* (New York: Random House, 2005), 5.

3. Eckhart Tolle, *The Power of Now* (Novato, CA: New World Library, 2000), 15.

4. Toni Packer, *The Wonder of Presence* (Boston: Shambhala Press, 2002), 4.

5. An audio file of this guided process, recorded by the author, can be downloaded at MysticCool.com.

6. Eckhart Tolle, *The Power of Now* (Novato, CA: New World Library, 2000), 17.

7. Thich Nhat Hahn, *Peace Is Every Step* (New York: Bantam Books, 1991), 11.

8. An audio file of this guided process, recorded by the author, can be downloaded at MysticCool.com.

9. Worksheets for this exercise can be downloaded at MysticCool.com.

10. Martin Seligman, PhD, *Learned Optimism, How to Change Your Mind and Your Life* (New York: Free Press, 1990), 221.

11. Joel Osteen, *Become a Better You: 7 Keys to Improving Your Life Every Day* (New York: Simon & Schuster, 2007), 117.

CHAPTER 10

1. Al Siebert, PhD, *The Survivor Personality* (New York: Perigee Books, 1996).

Notes

2. M. Fenton-O'Creevy, N. Nicholson, E. Soane, and P. Willman, "Trading on Illusions: Unrealistic Perceptions of Control and Trading Performance," *Journal of Occupational and Organizational Psychology* 76 (2003): 53–68.

3. Gangaji, *The Diamond in Your Pocket* (Boulder: Sounds True, 2007), 177.

4. An audio file of this guided process, recorded by the author, can be downloaded at MysticCool.com.

5. Eckhart Tolle, *The Power of Now* (Novato, CA: New World Library, 2000), 56.

6. Steve Hagen, *Buddhism Plain and Simple* (New York: Broadway Books, 1977), 16–17.

7. An audio file of this guided process, recorded by the author, can be downloaded at MysticCool.com.

CHAPTER 11

1. Louis Cozolino, *The Neuroscience of Human Relationships* (New York: W. W. Norton, 2006), 5.

2. S. Y. Bookheimer, M. Dapretto, M. S. Davies, M. Iacoboni, J. H. Pfeiffer, A. A. Scott, and M. Sigman, "Understanding Emotions in Others: Mirror Neuron Dysfunction in Children with Autism Spectrum Disorder," *Nature Neuroscience* 9, no. 1 (2006): 28–30; V. Gallese, "The Roots of Empathy: The Shared Manifold Hypothesis and the Neural Basis of Intersubjectivity," *Psychopathology* 36 (2003): 171–180.

3. Robert Sapolsky, "Why Zebras Don't Get Ulcers: The Devastating Effects of Stress on Children," Keynote address, Brain Connection to Education Spring Conference, San Francisco (May 11–13, 2000): http://cklrecords.blogspot.com/2006/03/why-zebras-dont-get-ulcers.html.

4. Erich Fromm, *The Art of Loving* (New York: Harper Perennial, 1989), 8.

5. Helen Fisher, *The Science of Love, and the Future of Women*, Mp4 recording (Ted Conferences, LLC, 2006): http://www.ted.com/index.php/talks/helen_fisher_tells_us_why_we_love_cheat.html.

Notes

6. J. Bruhn, "An Epidemiological Study of Myocardial Infarctions in an Italian-American Community," *Journal of Chronic Disease* 18 (1967): 353–357.

7. John Bruhn and Stewart Wolf, *The Roseto Story* (Norman, OK: University of Oklahoma Press, 1979), 41.

8. Kathleen A. Brehony, PhD, *Living a Connected Life: Creating and Maintaining Relationships* (New York: Holt, 2003), 48.

9. George Santayana, *The Works of George Santayana* (New York: Charles Scribner's Sons, 1932), 62.

10. Tara L. Gruenewald, Reagan A. R. Gurung, Laura Cousino Klein, Brian P. Lewis, Shelley E. Taylor, and John A. Updegraff, "Biobehavioral Responses to Stress in Females: Tend-and-Befriend, Not Fight-or-Flight," University of California, Los Angeles, *Psychological Review* 107, no. 3 (2000): 411–429.

11. University Of California Los Angeles, "UCLA Researchers Identify Key Biobehavioral Pattern Used By Women To Manage Stress," *Science Daily* (May 22, 2000): http://www.sciencedaily.com/releases/2000/05/000522082151.htm.

12. "Social Support, Stress, and the Common Cold: A Summary of a Presentation by Sheldon Cohen, PhD of Carnegie Mellon University: NIH Record—1997," *Psychological Science* 14, no. 4 (2003): 320–327.

13. S. L. Brown, R. M. Nesse, D. M. Smith, and A. D. Vinokur, "Providing Social Support May Be More Beneficial than Receiving It: Results from a Prospective Study of Mortality," *Psychological Science* 14, no. 4 (2003): 320–327.

14. V. Gallese, "The Roots of Empathy: The Shared Manifold Hypothesis and the Neural Basis of Intersubjectivity," *Psychopathology* 36 (2003): 171–180.

15. Ker Than, "Scientists Say Everyone Can Read Minds," *LiveScience* (April 27, 2006): http://www.livescience.com/health/050427_mind_readers.html.

16. Daniel Goleman, "Friends For Life: An Emerging Biology of Emotional Healing," *The New York Times* (October 10, 2006).

Notes

17. J. K. Kiecolt-Glaser and T. L. Newton, "Marriage and Health: His and Hers," *Psychological Bulletin* 127, no. 4 (2001): 472–503.

18. Carl Rogers, *The Carl Rogers Reader*, ed. Howard Kirschenbaum and Valerie Land Henderson, 3rd ed. (New York: Houghton-Mifflin, 1989), 135–136.

19. Carl R. Rogers, *A Way of Being* (New York: Houghton Mifflin, 1980), 115–116.

20. Ibid., 116.

21. Ibid., 117.

22. Gregory Harper and Brad Johnson, *Becoming a Leader the Annapolis Way* (New York: McGraw-Hill Professional, 2004), 178.

23. An audio file of this guided process, recorded by the author, can be downloaded at MysticCool.com.

24. Exercise codeveloped by Cheryl Geoffrion.

CHAPTER 12

1. Philip Rieff, *Freud: The Mind of the Moralist* (New York: Viking Press, 1979), 59.

2. Henry H. Lamberton, "Carl Rogers' View of Personal Wholeness," Paper, Institute for Christian Teaching, Faculty of Religion, Loma Linda University, Loma Linda, CA (1993).

3. Carl Rogers, *The Carl Rogers Reader*, ed. Howard Kirschenbaum and Valerie Land Henderson, 3rd ed. (New York: Houghton-Mifflin, 1989), 381.

4. Ibid., 380.

5. Ibid., 420.

6. Ibid., 413.

7. Visit http://www.chapters.indigo.ca/books/Now-Discover-Your-Strengths-Marcus-Buckingham-Donald-O-Clifton/9780743201148-item.html.

8. Marcus Buckingham and Donald O. Clifton, *Now, Discover Your Strengths* (New York: Free Press, 2001), 6–8.

9. Ibid., 12.

Notes

10. Marianne Williamson, *A Return to Love: Reflections on the Principles of a Course in Miracles* (San Francisco: HarperCollins, 1992), 190.

11. Thomas Merton, *The Intimate Merton*, ed. Patrick Hart and Jonathan Montaldo (San Francisco, 1996), 161.

12. Worksheets for this exercise can be downloaded at MysticCool.com.

13. Visit MysticCool.com to learn more about offered workshops, personal coaching, and read Don Goewey's blog for updates on events.

14. Diana Abitz, Patrick Dobson, and Charles McGuire, *The Best Advice Ever for Teachers* (Roseburg, OR: Andrews McMeel Publishing, 2001), 82.

15. Marcus Buckingham, *One Thing You Need to Know* (New York: Simon & Schuster, 2005), 272.

EPILOGUE

1. Richard G. Klein, *The Dawn of Human Culture* (New York: Nevraumont Publishing Co., 2002), 133.

2. Marshall Rosenberg, *Speak Peace* (Encinitas, CA: PuddleDancer Press, 2005), 131.

3. Ernest Holmes, *The Science of Mind* (New York: Dodd, Meade & Company, 1938), 306.

4. Gerald Jampolsky, MD, *Love Is Letting Go of Fear* (Berkeley: Celestial Arts, 1975), 123.

5. Dalai Lama XIV, "Never Give Up," *The Global Network Against Weapons & Nuclear Power in Space* (July 1, 2001): http://seniorspeace .mennonite.net/Dalai_Lama.html.

Index

acceptance, 157–159

adaptive decision making, 19–20

ah-ha experiences, 35–37, 102, 144–145

AIDS/HIV, xxiii–xxiv

Alexander the Great,

Allure of Toxic Leaders, The (Lipman-Blumen), 41

American Psychological Association, 7

amygdala
overview, 43–59
attentional bias for threat, 54
as compared with neocortex, 48–49
conditioned response, 53
as fear center, 40–41, 45–46, 51–52, 55–56
hippocampus, working with, 58–59, 69

militant nature of, 57
role in chronic stress, 65
in stress response, 43–51

Andrew's story, 99–100

anxiety
attacks of, 86
general, 55
incidence of, 64
separateness, 127, 147–148, 165–166

anxiety attacks, 86

Apollo. *See also* neocortex
as compared with Mars, 28, 47, 57, 65–66
creative intelligence, 27–28
executive functions, 28–31, 48
fear, 41, 43
in mythology, 27–28, 35

Aristotle, 2, 168

artificial intelligence, 34

Index

attention, 78–79, 125

attentional bias for threat, 54

attitude. *See also* dynamically peaceful attitude

  attitudinal healing, 79

  of calm, 77, 137–138

  negative, 60–61, 72, 103–105, 132–135, 180

  as neuroplastic, 11

  positive, 1–4, 78–79, 157–158

  power of, 108–109

  PreAttitude, 145–146

Australian aboriginals, 14

authentic self, 165–167

autonomic nervous system, 28

awareness

  of fear factors, 100–102

  guided imagery, 90–92, 96–98

  of negative tendencies, 86, 103–105, 145, 180

  as quality of Mystic Cool, 83

  of stress factors, 89–99

Awareness (de Mello), 102

Barton, Harrison, 111

beautiful mind, 6, 41, 82

Become a Better You (Osteen), 135

better angels, 28–29, 57

Binet, Alfred, 68–69

brain. *See also* brain function; emotional brain; mind

  evolution, 1–2, 37–39, 83–84

  immutable, 67–69

  intelligence, 31–34, 45

  mind–brain connection, 67–69, 72–75, 122–123

  mystical, 67

  primitive, 13–25

  reptilian brain, 13

  three gods of neurology, 11–12, 19, 28. *See also* Apollo; Dragon; Mars

brain function. *See also* amygdala; neocortex

  hippocampus, 58–59, 69

  hormones, 59–60

  memory, 58–59

  motor cortex, 70

  neurogenesis, 59

  neuroplasticity, 11, 65–66, 119–124

  neurotoxicity, 54–55, 58

  optimal, xxviii, 30–32

  orbitofrontal cortex, 70

  prefrontal cortex, 19–20, 28–31, 73–76, 123

  stress effects, xxviii, 6, 8–9, 50, 103–105

  Tibetan monk study, 74–78, 83

Bryner, Jeanna, 61

Buckingham, Marcus, 173

Buddha/farmer parable, 141–142

Buddhism. *See also* Dalai Lama

  eighty-fourth problem, 141–142

  Tibetan monk study, 74–78, 83

"Building Up to a Meltdown" (*Los Angeles Times*), 86

bumble bees, 14–15

Index

Cacioppo, John, 154
calm, attitude of, 77, 137–138
Calvinism, 156
Campbell, Joseph, 42
Camus, Albert, 40, 55
Candy, John, 111
Cather, Willa, 49–50
Center for Attitudinal Healing ("the Center"), xxii–xxvi
chicken soup, 152–153
children
    parental relationships, 30, 61–63, 68
    stress in, 63–64, 151
Chingachgook, 16–17
chronic stress, 7–8, 58–66, 147–148
Civilization and Its Discontent (Freud), 167
Clear Button, 129–130
Clear Mind, Wild Heart (Whyte), 114
cognitive behavioral therapy (CBT), 72
communication. *See also* listening
mental, 113–114
mirror neuron system, 153–159
resonance, 28, 154–159
compassion, xix, 162–164
conditioned response, 53
consciousness
conscious mind, xviii–xix, 27
    evolution of, 33–35, 83–84, 176
    expansion, 35
    flow states, 5–6, 10–11, 31–33, 143–145

stream of, 126–129
control, 138–141
Control Exercise, 139–140
Cooper, Andrew, 32–33
cortisol, 62–63
Course in Miracles, A (Schucman), 105
Craig, Jenny, 62
creative intelligence, 27–28
crimes of passion, 55–56
Critical Voice, 133–135, 180
Csikszentmihalyi, Mihaly, 10, 90
cultural prescience, 21–22

Dalai Lama
    on mind–brain connection, 67, 69, 72
    Tibetan monk study, 73–75
    on working for peace, 178
Damasio, Antonio, 19–20
Davidson, Richard, 73–76
de Mello, Anthony, 102–105
decision making
    adaptive, 19–20
    neocortex, 36
    premature, 58
    resonance, 140–141
Dement, William, xxi
depression
    clinical, 74
    examples, 64–65
    treatment of, 70–73, 86, 123
Diogenes,
directional tendency, 167–168

Index

discipline, 120

distress, 87

dopamine, 60

Dordogne Valley, 38–39

Dragon
heart intelligence, 20–21, 32
in mythology, 13–14
nature of, 13–14, 19–20
primitive brain, 13–25
survival instinct, 15

drakein, 13

dread, 49, 70

dynamically peaceful attitude
attributes, 108–109, 115, 179
power of, 31, 114–117, 125–126,
144–145
as unifying, xxviii, 11

eighty-fourth problem, 141–142

Einstein, Albert
flow states, 33
on intellect, 22
on the mystical, 19, 31
on red-pencil world, 166

Ekman, Paul, 74

Emerson, Ralph Waldo, 33, 176–177

emotional brain. See also mind-
made reality
overview, 43–66
balance, 28–29
fear, 40–42, 155
heart connection, 20–21
intelligence, 21, 131
memory, 46–47, 53

moodiness, 56–57
world view, 102

Emotional Intelligence (Goleman),
154

emotional memory, 46–47, 53

emotional negativity, 60–61,
103–105, 132–135

emotions. See also emotional
brain; fear
balance, 28–29
crimes of passion, 55–56
fight-or-flight response, 45–48,
53, 152
joy, 2–4, 144
negative, 60–61, 103–105, 132–135
positive, 1–4
thoughts and, 51–52

empathic understanding, 158–159

empathy, 29, 41, 158–159

End of Stress as We Know It, The
(McEwen), 6

"enriched environment," 18

entropy, psychic, 10–11

Eriksson, Peter, 69

eudaimonia, 2

eustress, 8–9

evil, 39–42, 156

Evil Genes (Oakley), 40–41

extension, 79, 83

external goals, 142–143

eye of the storm. See also flow states
overview, 107–117
locating, 9–11, 119
qualities of, 4, 87

Index

Falstaff, 23
family,61–63, 68, 150–151
Family and Work Institute, 61
fault finding, 78, 166, 169–171
fear. *See also* stress
    amygdala (fear center in brain),
        40–41, 45–46, 51–52, 55–56
    anxiety, 55, 64, 86, 103, 148
    attentional bias for threat, 54
    causes of, xvi–xviii, 6, 100–102
    as compared with fears,
        xxiv–xxv
    dread, 49, 70
    emotional brain, 40–42, 155
    emotional memory, 46–47, 53
    forgiveness and, 159–160
    hairpin trigger fear, 55–56
    letting go of, 79–81
    of our own power, 171
    primal fear, 45–49
    primal v. psychological, 52
    psychological, 51–57
    as reactive intelligence, 45, 47
    refuted, 100–103
    threat, 35, 46–50, 54
"Feel It to Heal It" exercise, 96–98
feelings. *See also* emotions
    gut feelings, 19–20, 29
    positive, 60
    relaxation exercise, 96–98
    stress reactions, 50–52
fight-or-flight response, 45–48, 53,
    152
Fisher, Helen, 148

flow states
    as compared with psychic
        entropy, 10–11
    as optimal, xxviii, 5–6, 31–33,
        143–145
foresight, 21–22, 25
forgiveness
    importance of, 159–160
    nature of, 160
    as process, 161–162
    release exercise, 163–164
    willingness, 161–162
formative tendency, 167
Frankl, Viktor, 109, 111–114
Franz, Ivory, 69
Freud, Sigmund, 167
Fromm, Erich, 148
fully functioning person, 23, 28,
    169, 170

$GABA_A$ receptors, 29
Galinsky, Ellen, 61
Gallup Organization annual survey,
    6–7
gamma wave activity, 9
Gandhi, Mahatma 12, 21, 82, 176
Gangaji, 138
Gardner, Howard, 5
Gaziantep Museum, 43
Gazzaniga, Michael S., 68
genetics, 40–41
genius, 1–12, 39
genuineness, 157–158
giving, 148, 153

Index

Goethe, Johann Wolfgang von, 3, 4
Goleman, Daniel, 75, 154
good life. *See also* dynamically
    peaceful attitude
  overview, 1–7
  key to, 42, 73, 83, 87
  as process, 168–169
  Tibetan monk study, 73–74
Gould, Elizabeth, 69
Greeks, classical, 2, 13–14, 27–28,
    30, 35
guided imagery, 90–92, 96–98
gut feelings, 19–20, 29

Hafiz, 163–164
Hahn, Thich Nhat, 129
hairpin trigger fear, 55–56
hate, 49–50
Hawkeye, 16
Hawkins, Jeff, 34
heart, 20–22, 32, 153
Hebb, Donald, 69
Heschel, Abraham Joshua, 6, 12
high illusion of control, 138
hippocampus, 58–59, 69
HIV/AIDS, xxiii–xxiv
Holocaust survivors, 111–114
Homo sapiens, 38
hormones
  dopamine, 60
  growth, 147–148
  oxytocin, 152
  serotonin, 59–60
  tryptophan, 60

human being, classic archetype,
    23–25
humanistic psychology, 23, 79. *See
    also* Rogers, Carl R.

Iacoboni, Marco, 153
immutable brain, 67–69
incessant thinking, 126–129
inner peace, xviii–xx, 143–146
inner stance, 79
inner vision, xxi–xxii
inner-directed mind, 17–18
insight
  ah-ha experiences, 35–37, 102,
    144–145
  as inner guide, 25
  mechanism of, 29
instinct, 13–15
intelligence
  artificial, 34
  creative, 27–28
  emotional, 21, 131
  in productive harmony, 31–32
  reactive, 45, 47
  zone, 32–33
intuition, 19–20, 25, 29

Jampolsky, Gerald, xxii, 143,
    177
Jastrow, Robert, 83
Jesus, 22, 121
Jobs, Steve, 25
Jordan, Michael, 32
joy, 2–4, 144

Index

Joyce, James, 42
judgment, 130–131, 161
judgments, 130–132

Kabat-Zinn, Jon, 75–76
Kandel, Erik, 4
Katie, Byron, 126
Kazantzakis, Nikos, 23–25
Kekulé, Friedrich, 33
Kell, William, 151
Kennedy, John F., 173, 176
Kierkegaard, Søren, xvii, 143
King, Martin Luther Jr., 129

Lasky, Karl, 69
Last of the Mohicans, The (film),
    16–17
Lawrence, D. H., 6
Lazarus, Richard, 88
LeDoux, Joseph, 48, 53
Lipman-Blumen, Jean, 41
listening
    genuine, 155–156, 158
    as noetic art, 20
    to self within, 33, 158–159, 169
Loizaga, Alberto, xxv–xxvi
longevity, 151–153
love, 147–151, 159–160
Love is Letting Go of Fear
    (Jampolsky), 177
Lubie's story, xxvi–xxvii

Making a Wish exercise, 121
malignant narcissists, 40–41

Mangar-kunjer-kunja, 14
Mars. *See also* emotional brain
    overview, 43–66
    as compared with Apollo, 28, 47,
        57, 65–66
    dread, 49
    mind-made reality, 102, 130–131
    in mythology, 13, 43
    reactive power, 43, 65
    stress reactions, 57–58
    world view, 102
Maslow, Abraham, 167
May, Rollo, xvii, 3
Mayberg, Helen, 72
McEwen, Bruce, 6
meditation, 31, 72–79. *See also*
    mindfulness; visualization
memory, 46–47, 53, 58–59
Mendeleyev, Dmitri, 33
Menninger, Karl, 109
mental practice, 69–73
Merton, Thomas, 171
Merzenich, Michael, 69
Milgram, Stanley, 41–42
military leadership qualities, 159
Miller, Earl K., 19
mind. *See also* mind-made reality
    beautiful, 6, 41, 82
    conscious mind, xviii–xix, 27
    inner-directed, 17–18
    mind–body connection, xviii, 9,
        75, 109
    mind–brain connection, 67–69,
        72–75, 122–123

Index

mind, *continued*
  mindfulness, 72–79, 83, 123
  outer-directed, 16–17
Mind and Life Institute, 67
mind–body connection, xviii, 9, 75, 109
mind–brain connection, 67–69, 72–75, 122–123
Mindful Brain, The (Siegel), 28–30, 122–123
mindfulness, 72–79, 123. *See also* Mystic Cool
Mindfulness Awareness Research Center, xxvi
mindfulness-based stress reduction, 76–78, 123
mind-made reality
  critical voice, 133–135
  distorted, 125
  illusions, 52, 102
  judgments, 130–132
  negative, 71–72
mirror neuron system, 153–159
Mis Misa, 80
monk study (Tibetan)
  overview, 74–78
  attitudes, 77
  brain function, 74–78, 83
  good life, 73–74
  lovingkindness, 77
  mindfulness, 76–78, 83
  one-pointedness, 76–77
  thangka visualization, 78
Montana, Joe, 109–111

mood set point, 67–69, 73–74, 76
moodiness, 56–57
morality, 29, 40–42
Mother Teresa, 175
motor cortex, 70
Mount Shasta, 79–81
Moyers, Bill, 42
My Ántonia (Cather), 49–50
My Life and the Beautiful Game (Pelé), 32
Mystic Cool
  overview, 11, 78–81
  attitude, 78–79
  qualities of, 81–83, 125, 137, 165
  steps to, 82–83
  as the zone, 107–108
mythology, 13–14, 27–28, 35, 43

National Institutes of Health study, 152–153
Native Americans, 14, 16–17, 19
natural world, 43–45
Nazi camps, 111–114
Neanderthals, 38
negative self-image, 132–133
negative self-talk, 132–135
negative thinking, 72, 103–105
negentropy, psychic, 10
neocortex
  overview, 27–42
  as compared with amygdala, 48–49
  in decision making, 36
  evolution of, 1–2, 33–39
  function, 11, 19, 35–37

Index

nervous system, 28
neurocompetitive advantage, 10
neurogenesis, 59, 69
neurology
   "enriched environment," 18
   three gods of, 11–12, 19, 28. *See also* Apollo; Dragon; Mars
neuroplasticity, 65, 69–70, 119–124
neuroscience, 67–69
neurotoxicity, 54–55, 58
Nicklaus, Jack, 90
Niebuhr, Reinhold, 138
nonlocality, 21
Now, Discover Your Strengths (Buckingham, Clifton), 170–171
Nurses' Health Study, 151–152

Oakley, Barbara, 40–41
obedience experiment, 41–42
obsessive-compulsive disorder (OCD), 70–71, 86, 123
Olerud, John, 32
On Intelligence (Hawkins), 34
One Thing You Need to Know (Buckingham), 173
one-pointedness, 76–77
Oradour-sur-Glane, 40
orbitofrontal cortex, 70
Ortega y Gasset, José, 121
Osteen, Joel, 135
Otto, Herb, 170–171
outer-directed mind, 16–17
overwhelm, 138, 141–143

oxytocin, 152

Packer, Toni, 127
parasympathetic nervous system, 28
parents, 61–63, 68
peace. *See also* dynamically peaceful attitude
   attaining, xxvi–xxvii, 80
   attitude of calm, 77, 137–138
   brain function and, xxviii, 29–32
   inner, xxviii, 143–146
   practicing, 119–124
   as psychological strength, 114
   qualities of, xxvii, 29–31
Pearce, Joseph Chilton, 20–21
Pelé, 32
person-centered approach, 156
PET scans, 71
Pilar's story, xxv–xxvi
Playing In the Zone (Cooper), 32–33
Poe, Nathaniel, 16
post-traumatic stress, xxvi, 90, 161
potato bin story, 167–168
Power of Myth, The (PBS), 42
Power of Now, The (Tolle), 80
practice
   mental, 69–73
   neuroplasticity of, 119–124
   of one-pointedness, 76–77
   as quality of Mystic Cool, 82–83
PreAttitude, 145–146
prefrontal cortex
   brain activity, 73–76, 123
   consciousness expansion, 35

Index

prefrontal cortex, *continued*
  executive functions, 28–31
  gut feelings, 19–20, 29
premonition, 21–22
prestimulus response, 21
Pribram, Karl, xxi
primal nature, 23–25, 45–49, 52. *See
    also* stress response system
primitive brain
  overview, 13–25
  body and, 15–16
  as instinctive, 13–15
  nature of, 13–15
  as outer-directed, 16–17
principle of relationship, 77–78
Prisoner's Dilemma, 59–60
ProAttitude, xxviii, 180, 182
projection, 132–133
psychic entropy, 10–11
psychic negentropy, 10
psychological fear, 51–57
psychological projection, 132–133
psychology. *See also* Rogers, Carl R.
  humanistic psychology, 23, 79
  person-centered approach, 156
  stress studies, 7
  views of human nature, 167

Quinn, Anthony, 24

Ramon y Cajal, Santiago, 68–69
rattlesnake encounters, 49–50
recovery, 166–167
red wine, 152–153

red-pencil world, 166–169
reframing, 145–146
relationship, principle of, 77–78
relationships
  eighty-fourth problem, 141–142
  forgiveness, 159–162
  influential, 170–171
  mirror neuron system, 153–159
  with nature, 43–44
  obstacles to, 147–151
  parental, 61–63, 68
  resonance in, 154, 156–159
reptilian brain, 13
resonance, 28, 154, 156–159
response flexibility, 29
Return to Love, A (Williamson), 171
Rizzollati, Giaccamo, 153
Robinson, Patsy, xxii–xxiii
Rogers, Carl R.
  overview, xx, xxii
  on awareness, 23
  formative tendency, 167–170
  person-centered approach, 156
  on resonance, 156–159
Rogers, Robert, 60
Roseto Effect, 149–151
Rousseau, Jean-Jacques, 23–24
Rumi, 128, 129

Sapolsky, Robert, 9, 51, 147–148
Scheer, Gene, 39
Schopenhauer, Arthur, 12
Schwartz, Jeffrey, 70–71, 79
Schwartz, Larry, 110

Index

Segal, Zindel, 72, 79
self-acceptance, 151, 158–159
self-actualizing tendency, 167–168, 171
self-righteousness, 57
Seligman, Martin, 133–134
Selye, Hans, 8–9, 65
separateness, 127, 147–148, 165–166
serenity prayer, 138
serotonin, 59–60
Shakespeare, William, 23, 126
Sherrington, Charles, 69
Signs of Stress exercise, 93–95
sidekicks, 23
Siebert, Al, 137
Siegel, Daniel, xxvi, 28–30, 122–123
Singletary, Mike, 110
somatic states, 19–20
Spiegel, David, xxi
Starks, John, 32
Stegner, Wallace, 44
stream of consciousness, 126–129
strength finding, 170–173
Strength Finding exercise, 172–173
stress. *See also* stress response
    system
  overview, 3–9
  awareness of, 89–99
  brain function, xxviii, 6, 8–9, 50, 103–105
  in children, 151
  chronic, 7–8, 58–66, 147–148
  as compared with stressors, 88–89
deconstructing events, 87–96, 139–140
demographics, 6–7, 63–66
  as a disease, 63
  distress, 87
  eustress, 8–9
  hormones, xxviii, 6, 8–9, 46–47, 50, 54
  as internal/subjective, 87–88
  mindfulness-based reduction in, 76–78
  mindfulness-based stress reduction, 123
  ordinary, 7
  origins of, xxvii–xxviii, 6, 50–52, 87–88
  patterns, 85–95
  physical manifestations, 96–99
  post-traumatic, xxvi, 90, 161
  transcending, 60–62, 65–66
stress hormones
  affect on brain function, xxviii, 6, 8–9, 50
  attentional bias for threat, 54
  in children, 151
  emotional memory, 46–47, 53
Stress of Life, The (Selye), 65
stress response system. *See also* stress
  amygdala, 43–51
  conditioned response, 53
  fight-or-flight, 45–48, 53, 152
  hormones, xxviii, 6, 8–9, 46–47, 50, 54

Index

stress response system, *continued*
  neurotoxicity, 54–55
  physiology of, 48–50
  primal fear, 45–49
  psychological fear, 51–57
stress tell, 95–96
Stressometer, 92–93
stressors, 88–89
striatum, 70
Stupski, Larry, xxvii–xxviii
Suddenly Last Summer (Williams),
  44
sympathetic nervous system, 28

Taylor, Shelley E., 152
thangka, 78
threat, 35, 46–50, 54
three gods of neurology, 11–12, 19,
  28. *See also* Apollo; Dragon;
  Mars
Tibetan monk study
  overview, 74–78
  attitudes, 77
  brain function, 74–78, 83
  good life, 73–74
  lovingkindness, 77
  mindfulness, 76–78, 83
  one-pointedness, 76–77
  thangka visualization, 78
Tolle, Eckhart
  on conflict, 140
  on external goals, 142
  on incessant thinking, 127
  on peace, xxvi–xxvii, 80

on sense of self, 76, 125,
  128–129
toxic leadership, 40–41
transparency, 157
tryptophan, 60

Uncas, 16
unconditional positive regard,
  157–158
understanding, empathic, 158–159

visualization. *See also* meditation
  guided imagery, 90–92, 96–98
  letting go, 177
  reframing, 145–146
  thangka visualization, 78

warriors, way of, 16–17
Watching the Thinker exercise,
  128–129
What's Stressing Me exercise,
  90–92
wholeness, 165–170
Why Zebras Don't Get Ulcers
  (Sapolsky), 51
Whyte, David, 114
Williams, Tennessee, 44
Williamson, Marianne, 171
Wolf Willow (Stegner), 44
work. *See also* stress
  dissatisfaction, xxvii–xxviii
  flow states, 5–6, 10–11, 31–33,
  143–145
  obedience experiment, 41–42

Index

red-pencil world, 166–169
worker psychological profiles,
 170–171
worry, 71, 116–117

Yalom, Irvin, xxi
Youngblood, Jack, 109–111

zebra analogy, 54–55
zone, 32–33, 107–108, 144
Zorba the Greek (Kazantzakis),
 23–25
Zorbas, Georgis, 24. *See also Zorba
 the Greek* (Kazantzakis)
Zsien, Joe, 53